OVER THE PL_

PART TWO

PEAKDALE TO MILLERS DALE

A Midland 7ft compound 4-4-0 1028 climbs towards Peak Forest Jct.with a lightweight down express. This picture says it all, magnificent scenery, a railway which has blended into that scenery to a point where it looks as if it always has been there. A classic view of a Midland Rly loco doing just what it was built for.

COMPILED & WRITTEN BY
J. M. BENTLEY

ISBN 978-1-909625-00-6

Published in the United Kingdom by Book Law Publications
382 Carlton Hill, Nottingham NG4 1JA

Printed by The Amadeus Press, Cleckheaton, BD19 4TQ

ACKNOWLEDGEMENTS

As with volume one, I am indebted to many people for the assistance given with the compiling of this volume. Glynn Waite for turning up with many interesting photographs and train tickets. The Rowsley Association for allowing their material to be used.

The Manchester Locomotive Society for allowing photographs from their extensive collection to be used. Trevor Moseley for allowing his signalling diagrams to be copied for use in this book and also for the trouble he took over the history of the making of concrete signal posts by the M&GNR Rly.

To Eddie Johnson for printing and providing many interesting photographs.

To my son Chris for photographing the scene as it is now and to Martin Dowling, a Director at Tunstead Quarry now owned by La Farge-Tarmac for arranging and allowing Chris to photograph within the works. To Frank Emmerson for the help and use of the images from the old ICI archive.

To Steve Allsop for photographs taken around Rusher Cutting tunnel. John Morten, as always, for allowing the use of his fathers photographs. Mike Fell for answering industrial loco questions. Thanks to Eric Ellis for the loan of the loco casualty reports.

Also I feel I ought to mention the staff at Amadeus Press, who have dealt with all my requirements and questions in a most business like manner. The hospitality shown by them has made us feel "at home" and their willingness to help has been greatly appreciated.

Tunstead Northwich 8F 2-8-0 48045 lifts its train of 16 bogie hoppers out of the siding onto the main line on a wet and miserable day in the mid 1950s. Assisted in the rear by a Buxton 4F 0-6-0 probably 44339, the regular loco for this job. ***Photo E Johnson collection***

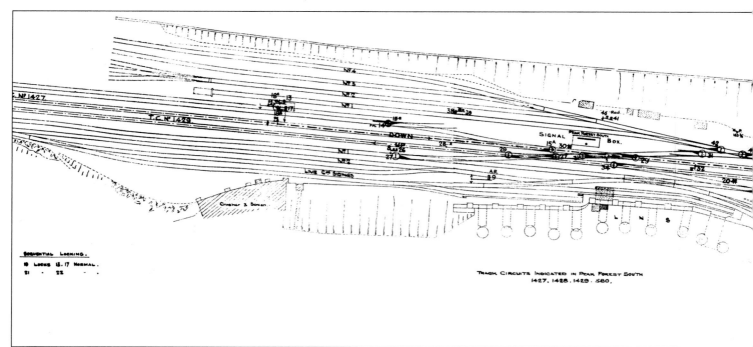

SEQUENTIAL LOCKING.

19 LOCKS 18. 17 NORMAL.
21 " 22 " "

TRACK CIRCUITS INDICATED IN PEAK FOREST SOUTH
1427. 1428. 1429. 580.

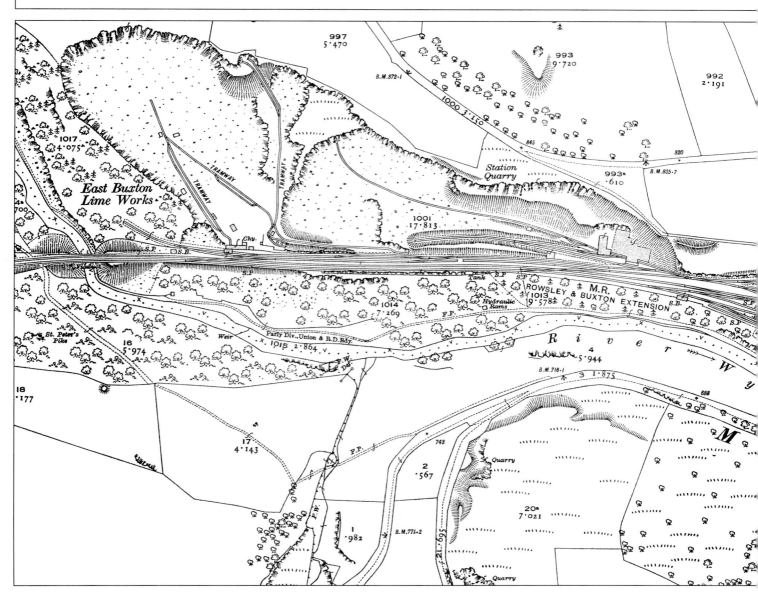

East Buxton
Lime Works

Peak Forest

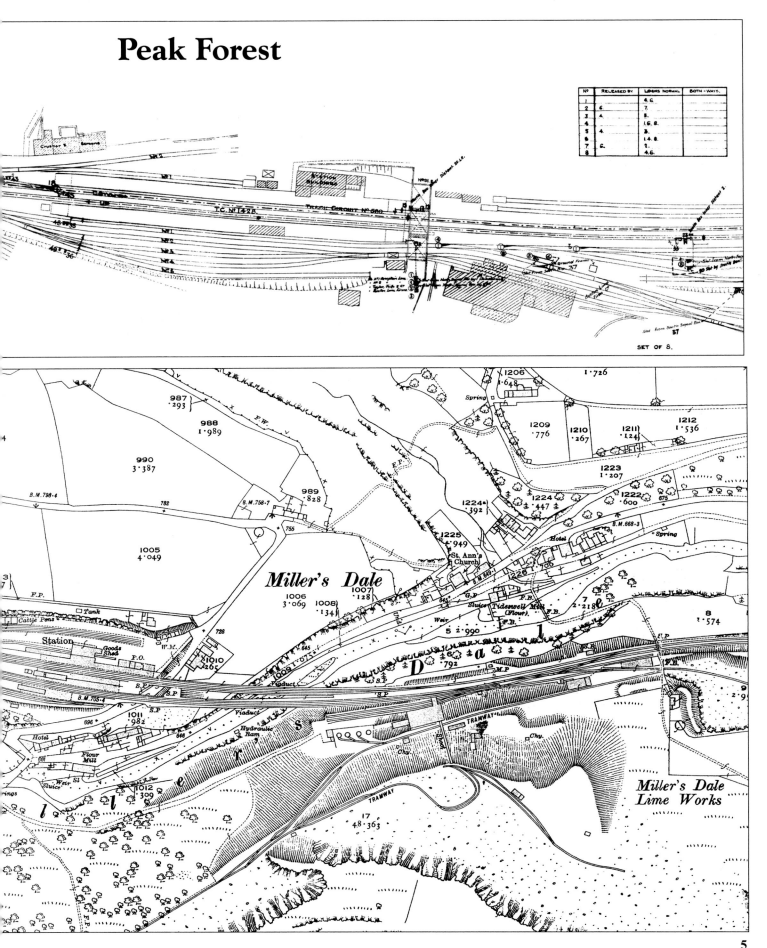

INTRODUCTION

In the first volume, which dealt with the line from Chinley to Peakdale, the amount of new photographic material found was quite amazing. Part two looks set to equal this, with many hitherto unseen photographs within its pages, a good number from the old ICI archive.

Having dealt in detail with Dove Holes tunnel in part one, the first thing which happened after publication, was the arrival of yet more photographs of the tunnels construction, and a fine set of photographs taken inside the tunnel during recent engineering works. So Part two commences with a further look back at this tunnel and not at Peak Forest South as planned.

Great emphasis has been placed on the quarrying industry, which still is the life blood of what is left of the line. Gone are the expresses and slow passenger trains, through freight such as coal also long gone, but quarries still remain. Not as many as in the old days, but far larger and more mechanized than their predecessors were.

A section of the book has been given over to the ICI steam and diesel locos, the service they gave to the industry was spread over many years and still continues. Quite a few pictures of the internal parts of the works are included.

Members of the public saw very little of the intestines of this massive enterprise, only a fleeting glance of the sidings or any activity near to the main line. The ICI policeman saw to that.

I am glad that during my footplate days I took quite a lot of pictures in the sidings at Tunstead, a miserable, noisy place for a young fireman to be, especially on a Saturday night waiting to bank the 10/46pm Northwich hoppers.

The never ending roar of the crusher, a sound that only an LMS 5XP on a down express could drown. When the crusher was stopped the silence was "deafening".

At Blackwell Mill one of the other ICI quarries was situated, known as South Works or South Central Works. With a very cramped sidings space. Its four kiln chimneys adding much to the overall blacking out of the district. Nothing now remains of this quarry, much hard work has gone into trying to erase this blot on the landscape with some considerable success.

We now enter the picturesque part of the line, clinging to the rock face above Chee Dale. It was found necessary to build three tunnels here. The first, Rusher Cutting tunnel, followed by Chee Tor No 2 and Chee Tor No1 which bring us to Millers Dale, not without passing yet another quarry East Buxton or Station Quarry, long since closed and where "Mother Nature" has been in control for many years.

Millers Dale station, originally a normal two line affair, was doubled in size in the early years of the twentieth century, necessitating the building of another viaduct alongside the original one to accommodate the two new lines.

Like Chinley, a very large station in the middle of nowhere was erected, and proudly named Millers Dale for Tideswell a village some miles away.

The stations main use was the connecting point for the Buxton services and the overtaking place for expresses and the preceding slow train services.

The original main line only went to Buxton, so all services started and ended there, but when the main line was extended to Manchester, the Buxton line became "the branch" and the well remembered connecting services from Millers Dale to Buxton began. Originally with the loco running round at each end, a system which remained until Pull and Push working was introduced in the 1930s.

Now it has all gone, instead of a complete closure, a severe pruning would have left us with a much needed service southwards. A direct link for the north-west into St Pancras for the Euro-Link services and a route down which heavy freight could be directed at night, relieving our atrocious roads of some of the heavy traffic they bear now.

Dove Holes Tunnel

This shows the sinking of No5 shaft above Dove Holes village. Not a great deal of "hi tech" machinery in view. The spoil heap in the background still exists, although much grown over now.

The troublesome north-end cutting. Whether or not this view was taken before or after the landslip which caused the lengthening of the tunnel is hard to tell. The general watery conditions are apparent in this picture.

I feel that this picture was taken after one of the numerous roof collapses at the north end. The brickwork looks as if it has been in for some while. The track has been slewed across to the centre of the tunnel and just enough headroom left for wagons to be placed underneath. After work was completed, I wonder if the track was left in this formation whilst the roof settled or fell in again. This might explain why a signal-box of sorts was placed within the tunnel for a short time.

Pictures of the recent work carried out in the tunnel to try and improve the drainage by employing a much deeper drain in an attempt to prevent flooding.

Modern equipment is in the forefront, no shovels or tilley lamps, but electric light, mechanical diggers and every other type of modern aid required.

The view of the ventilator shaft shows some of the work which has been done to try and lessen the continuous downpour on to the track below. A drainage ring has been put around inside the vent in an attempt to catch as much water as possible and pipe it down into the drains.

A class 66 loco stands shut down on the down gradient end of a train of long wheelbase spoil wagons.

The last picture shows just how much water there is to be drained away. The flow looks more like what one would expect in the Severn tunnel, not from a tunnel nearly 1300 feet above sea level. This is just part of the watershed from Cowlow.

A view of the construction of Peak Dale station in 1864. An aged contractors loco and wagons stand on what will eventually become the up main line. The first stages of the construction of the station are evident on the left of the picture. A row of primitive quarry cottages, high up on the right of the picture stand where the Buxton Lime Firms buildings were eventually placed. ***Photo Author's collection***

The station staff pose for the photographer in 1914. Quite a large staff was required here because of the amount of office work created by the quarries and their shipments by rail. Everything was written in ledgers by hand, so amongst the porters would be quite a few clerks. 28 young men from Peak Dale died in the 1914-1918 war, including a couple on this photograph, a large sacrifice from a small community.

Photo Author's collection

A trio of views of the daily life on the railway at Peak Dale in 1965.

A Rowsley class 9F 2-10-0 92051 passes through with an up fully fitted goods train. This class of loco was well suited to this work, their good riding qualities appreciated by the crews.

On rail-side shunting is in operation, this view shows the theatre signal very clearly. Wagons are being drawn off the ICI grinding plant road in preparation for marshalling into a train of empties for Great Rocks.

The loco carrying out these moves is Buxton 8F 2-8-0 48748 working the Peak Forest shunter diagram. Whilst this is happening, the down Northwich hoppers pass by banked by another Buxton 8F 2-8-0 48465. Above 48465's tender can be seen the remains of the Peep o'Day kilns, like everything else long gone.

Photos
J W Sutherland Manchester Loco Society

This old ICI picture of the station yard shows just how short of space the system was. The buildings on the left of the picture are part of the Bold Venture quarry loading arrangements. All the other roads are full to capacity with wagons which have been loaded or are waiting to be loaded. Clearances for loco movements are very narrow indeed, and those persons working on the ground would have to be very mindful of the lack of room.

Photo La Farge / Tarmac

24th January 1958. Heaton Mersey depots 48429 pulls slowly out of Peak Forest yard with the Runcorn cov-hop train on a rather snowy day. This train, which usually started from Tunstead sidings will have been tripped up to Peak Forest during the day by the trip loco. By starting the train from here the necessity for a banking loco will have been dispensed with.

Photo La Farge / Tarmac

Peak Forest South July 27th 1964 Northwich based 8F 2-8-0 48717 pounds the last yards to the summit of the bank with the 11.15 hoppers ex Tunstead Sidings. Very soon the Type 2 diesels will take over these diagrams and the class 8Fs will only appear to cover diesel failures. When this picture was taken this class of loco had been the regular motive power on these turns for 26 years, and had given very reliable service.

Photo J.M Bentley

A view from where a great deal of engine spotting was done, the footpath leading from the station towards High Fields. A class 8F lifts a train of limestone out of the down goods line towards the summit. In the background are the remains of the Great Rocks quarry kilns and associated buildings, used by a local coach company as a garage. Now all swept away, only the houses on Great Rocks now remain.

Photo J W Sutherland Manchester Loco Society

The working over the Peak by the ex LNER B1 class became quite commonplace in the 1960s. 61170 of Doncaster depot is in charge of the morning Derby-Chinley stopping passenger train in the winter of 1962.

Photo J M Bentley

Peak Forest South May 28th 1964. A Newton Heath 8F 2-8-0 48774 pulls out of the down goods road with a Rowsley- Brewery sidings goods. This loco along with sister locos 48773 and 48775 came into BR ownership in the late 1950s, having been in War Department service until then. 48773 came to Buxton for a short while after coming down from Polmadie depot Glasgow where all three were originally allocated. 48774 did not come to Buxton but 48775 put in quite a bit of service with us until steam finished in 1968. All three could be easily identified by the W.D. double clack shut offs, the covers for which formed a saddle across the boiler top. Their other difference was that they were not fitted with exhaust injectors, but had two live steam types.

Photo J M Bentley

The down Northwich hoppers approach the South box headed by 48280 deputizing for a failed diesel loco on March 18th 1966. Banked in the rear by Buxton depot`s 48088. Class 8F 2-8-0s took over the banking duties from 4F 0-6-0s in the 1962/63 period. Buxton still had plenty of 4F locos to cover these turns, but when failed diesels had to be assisted, a regular occurrence at this time, a 4F was sorely taxed. At this time diesel failures were making the job a "laughing stock". The class 8Fs were able to shift a dead Sulzer and 10 coaches more easily than a 4F.

Photos J M Bentley

Peak Forest as it is now. A class 60 loco departs from the goods line, now used mainly as an extra sidings road with a train of 100 ton hopper wagons. Two class 66 locos are stabled in the sidings. This being the stabling place after the depot at Buxton was finished after privatization.

Photo Chris Bentley

A general view taken from Great Rocks quarry tip shows a very busy Peak Forest. A lengthy train of sheeted lime leaves the sidings for its journey north. On the down goods line a train of coal for Lancashire Steel at Irlam, all in private owner wagons awaits its turn to go down the bank. In the foreground three of the Long Sidings roads have loads of limestone, in ICI private owner wagons of varying sizes. In these days the wagons were loaded by hand or shute (the latter still requiring much man power).a lot of work for a lot of men. The picture also shows how congestion grew around places like Peak Forest. The holding of a through train like the one on the goods line, which no doubt, had one or more trains behind it whilst another train leaves the sidings, possibly for the Sheffield direction was regular practice. Next through would be an express, followed by a slow train. After all these had passed by, the coal train, if lucky, would get a run towards Cheadle Heath.

Photo La Farge / Tarmac

On May 16th 1962 one of the original batch of smaller fireboxed 8F 2-8-0s 48003 of Kirkby depot approaches Peak Forest with a down coal train banked in the rear by a 2-6-4T.

Photo W D Cooper

Ivatt 4MT 2-6-0 43048 is the motive power for a down coal train as it heads for the top of the bank on March 27th 1965. During the early 1960s Heaton Mersey depot collected quite a few of this class to replace the older 4F 0-6-0 types. The size of the Great Rocks tip can be appreciated in this picture. In the background the then new cement plant chimney can be seen nearing completion, now demolished in favour of a new plant further inside the quarry.

Photo J M Bentley

Long sidings March 18th 1966. The last time all the surviving ICI 5 plank wooden wagons were marshalled into a train, here seen just about to make their final journey down into the "field" at Great Rocks to be burned by the scrap metal men, who took away the remaining scrap. Driver Arthur Robinson watches the final preparations from the cab. 48744 was working the Peak Forest shunter turn. The two short arm signals above the train controlled the spot where the Long sidings No1 and 2 roads joined.

Photo J M Bentley

Halfway between Peak Forest South and Great Rocks Jct. 45689 "Ajax" passes under the now demolished bridge which linked Great Rock[s] quarry with the Upper End side of the valley. 45689 only made a short appearance on the Midland services when it was allocated to Traffor[d] Park depot on September 5th 1953 having been moved from Crewe North. It was reputedly transferred from Trafford Park to Longsigh[t] depot on September 19th, but here it is working an up express, still carrying a 9E shed plate on October 4th. Its working life finished o[n] December 12th 1964.

Photo E R Morte[n]

Great Rocks Jct. circa 1953. 45616 "Malta G.C." looking quite smart and no doubt just ex works roars past the "field" with a down expres[s] consisting of nine red and cream coaches. This loco remembered by all, was just about the most regular performer over the Peak, usuall[y] filthy dirty, but mechanically sound. In the last days of the 5XPs on these jobs this loco put up a wonderful performance on the 7.55am "Palatine" express to Manchester and succeeded in making one of the finest recorded runs over the Peak. This was after reaching 91 mph on the flat to Derby. When this run took place 45616 had done just 5,600 miles since its last overhaul a light intermediate, and was in good order. This run showed that with an interested crew, this class of loco could still hold its own amongst the class 7 types.

Photo Author's collection

Great Rocks Jct. July 4th 1960. The first down run of the down "Blue Pullman" photographed at 8/42pm by Ray Morten. To try and keep this train running to time and with no delays, it was worked under the double block system, which ensured two clear blocks ahead at all times.

The service had its share of set backs. Owing to its failure between Rowsley and Bakewell on one occasion it was assisted in the rear by a 4F 0-6-0 and train, much too every ones disgust. After a while the service was accelerated and on the first run, with the press and dignitaries on board, was heavily delayed at Monsal Dale by a freight train stuck in Headstones tunnel. Earlier in the day driver Clayton and fireman Taylor and guard Dawson were sent from Buxton with a "Crab" 2-6-0 to Millers Dale to work a train of empty wagons to Rowsley. This train had been put off there the previous night because Rowsley sidings could not deal with it.

At this time there was a 20 mph slack in Headstones tunnel on the up line owing to track relaying. On the way down the bank driver Clayton noticed that, for a train of empties they were taking rather a lot of holding. He entered Headstone tunnel at 20mph and with the gradient now against him opened the regulator to lift the train through, but the loco just sat down, no attempts to move had any success.

So, in accordance with working instructions, the train was split. The leading portion taken to Hassop, where it was put inside. The phones were now getting very hot indeed. Whilst putting off the leading portion, the fireman climbed on to the first wagon, only to find that it was loaded with heavy, flat steel ingots and not empty at all. The whole train was the same and empty labels had been put on by mistake.

Back tender first to Monsal Dale, where the "Pullman" was standing, with a lot of red faced officialdom on board. The "Crab" and crew, having collected the appropriate "wrong line order" proceeded on to the rear of the split train and dragged it back to Monsal Dale where it was put on the down line whilst the badly delayed "Pullman" got under way again.

I think it is fair to say that introduction of this train was brave attempt to modernize and speed up the services, in view of competition from internal air lines, but a railway like the Midland which was heavily used by slow moving freight, its signalling, mostly short block working, just did not lend itself to coping with high speed services, which needed many clear miles ahead of them.

Quite often Ray Morten would get inside information regarding the running of special trains. On this day, June 30th 1950, he and Harry Townley positioned themselves at Great Rocks to photograph a test train from Derby. Just preceding the special a down express was photographed headed by a filthy Kentish Town 5XP 45657 "Tyrwhitt". This loco was one of those which took part in exchange with 5XPs in Scotland, going to Perth in October 1952, thence to Carlisle Kingmoor depot in March 1953. 45657 returned to the L.M. region in the summer of 1962, when it was allocated to Bank Hall depot Liverpool. Withdrawal came in September 1964 from Patricroft depot.

Photo H Townley

The object of the trip out on that day in June 1950, was to photograph the new diesel electric loco 10800 on its first trip out over Peak Forest. It duly passed, a strange looking object for this era, but a shape with which we were to become quite used to seeing with the later day diesel classes. A joint venture between the North British Loco Co and British Thompson Houston, with H A Ivatt. The loco being designed for branch line work, It was fitted with a Davey-Paxman 16cyl 827 hp engine, and weighed in at nearly 70 tons.

Photo H Townley

Great Rocks 1932. An LMS 3cyl compound 4-4-0 1064 heads an up express past the quarry sidings. The uniform train sets of clerestory coaches have now given way to a "rag bag" mix of stock inherited by the LMS in 1923. The lower end of the sidings has been removed in readiness for the alterations needed to accommodate the new turntable soon to be built for the Northwich stone train programme. The double slip point will be replaced and the very badly positioned up home signal will become an upper quadrant job with a distant. At the time of this photograph Tunstead signal-box did not exist, so therefore the next block was Peak Forest Jct. a sufficient distance away so as not to need the short block distant signals. After the introduction of the new box at Tunstead it became necessary to apply distant signals to both home and starter signals at Great Rocks. When you look at this old signal, and bear in mind that all Midland locos were driven from the right side of the cab, little thought had gone into its positioning. It is on the left side of the track and is well away from the running line it controlled. All over the railway system there were badly positioned signals like this one, not too difficult to spot in fine weather conditions, but at night or in fog almost impossible to see. This picture shows what an area the Great Rocks quarry covered, soon to be replaced by the new Tunstead quarry.

Photo E R Morten

Great Rocks 2013. What a contrast to the previous picture. An E.W.S. class 66 loco crosses over for entry into the Great Rocks end of the Tunstead complex. Its train, consisting of 22 air braked bogie hoppers completes the modern scene. The background is unbelievable, trees now cover what was a busy quarry. The over bridge spanning the railway is also gone, along with the hundreds of men who worked in this quarry. Not only men did men work in these quarries, but so did women. Hannah Leach, a school friend of my mothers, was killed when the bulldozer she was driving plunged down the tip here at Great Rocks.

Photo Chris Bentley

22

Long sidings. The Great Rocks quarry was gradually closed down, as were Bold Venture and Perseverance quarries, leaving the ICI with Tunstead and Central Works Blackwell Mill as their main quarries. The closure of Great Rocks quarry enabled the sidings roads adjacent to the main line to be radically altered or removed. These two pictures show the gradual demolition of the site, no doubt greatly slowed down by the second World War. Both are interesting to compare with the later pictures. ***Photos La Farge / Tarmac***

Great Rocks 1960. Rowsley depot 9F 2-10-0 92049 restarts an up oil train after a signal check at the up home board. The reason for this check will be that a loco or locos will have preceded it and are crossing over the road from up to down at Tunstead on the way into the sidings. Thus as soon as all is clear both home and distant come off simultaneously. *Photo L.M Hobdey*

A busy moment at Great Rocks in 1958. A 4F 0-6-0 44461 of Workington depot, well off its beaten track, heads an up goods, whilst a down goods with a 4F banker climbs towards Peak Forest. The 8F in the foreground, having turned and taken water, awaits the time for its departure to Tunstead sidings for its return working to Northwich. *Photo L.M. Hobdey*

The Fell diesel loco 10100 heads an up express of ten coaches down the bank in the mid 1950s. The loco is in its altered wheel notation of 4-4-4-4 with the centre coupling rod removed. This loco put in a great deal of good work north of Derby and would no doubt have lasted longer if it had not suffered a serious fire at Manchester Central.   *Photo J Wooliscroft*

The up empty hoppers arrive behind Northwich 8F 48605. It is shown crossing over to gain entry to the ICI reception roads. The short arm signal controlling this move can be seen in the off position. This loco, like many others of the class, has been coupled to a Fowler 3500 gallon tender, which was for all concerned a very bad move. As well as loosing 500 gallons of water, the tenders were narrower than the loco, and instead of fire iron being kept within the tender, they were perched on top of the coal. As electrification progressed, fire irons in this position became a constant source of worry for loco crews. When the tender was fully coaled the fire irons were to close too the overhead wires for comfort.   *Photo J Wooliscroft*

The distance from Buxton to this vantage point, known as "Buxton Bridge" was about 3 miles. Like going to Peakdale station, it was at the bottom of rather a steep hill. All the younger engine spotters either walked there or more usually used their bicycles, but which ever form of transport used a very slow climb back to the top of the hill ensued. The men who took these photos arrived in style, John Wooliscroft owned an Austin Ruby, which had been the family vehicle since 1929. This little car still exists in the Coventry Motor Museum. Its progress back up the hill was not a deal faster than the boys on bicycles but more comfortable. The little car enabled John Wooliscroft and Len Hobdey to arrive to photograph the last up express, the 7/35pm ex Manchester Central. On this occasion in June 1959, 46154 "The Hussar" was caught working this turn during its very short stay at Kentish Town depot.

Photo J Wooliscroft

Same spot, same train, but this time under Pacific haulage. 70032 "Tennyson" is in charge of the train. The loco has just been transferred across Manchester from Longsight depot to Trafford Park along with its other shed mates 70031/33 after being displaced by diesels on the Euston jobs.   ***Photo W A Brown***

A Derby bound test train hauled by a Clayton "cab in the middle" diesel loco passes Great Rocks on its return trip from Chinley. All these locos had to do this round trip successfully before they could be accepted by British Railways. Whilst firing for Frank Bagshaw on the Peak Forest shunter, busy sorting out wagons in Tunstead sidings, the call came to go and assist a train stood at Millers Dale. We duly arrived there to find one of these locos on the test train of seven old suburban coaches stood on the down slow line. While I hooked on, Frank asked one of the "trilby hatted" officials what the problem was and how far did he want assisting. The loco with engine running, would not start the train, so we were instructed to assist to Peak Forest North, this we duly did. On arrival I got in between and uncoupled, back to Tunstead was the plan, but as we approached Peak Forest South, the signalman exhibited a red flag, and when we stopped, told us to go up to the rear of the test train and assist it over the summit as the loco was still incapable of moving it. We did not see the test train return.   ***Photo S Cameron***

Class 5MT 4-6-0 44938 approaches Great Rocks at the head of an up express on a cold looking February 14th 1953. A train of empty hoppers has been stabled in the up lay by, awaiting transfer into Tunstead for loading. Well known Buxton photographer Ray Morten is seen taking his shot from ground level. ***Photo H Townley***

A down express with a rebuilt Royal Scot 4-6-0 in charge 46122 "Royal Ulster Rifleman". Another of the class which only spent a month at Trafford Park depot (after transfer from Longsight) in May 1959. Going next to Upperby depot Carlisle where another short spell of a couple of weeks were spent, before coming south again to Bushbury depot. ***Photo J Wooliscroft***

Another train which, in mid summer, could be photographed at Great Rocks was the 4/35 ex St Pancras. The valley here was very deep and only when the sun was at its highest was there enough light amongst the deep shadows to get a good shot. On this occasion John Wooliscroft has succeeded in doing just that. Trafford Park depots 70021 "Morning Star" makes a fine sight as it climbs the last mile to the summit in the summer of 1958.

Great Rocks turntable January 2nd 1946. A Stanier "Crab" 2-6-0 2953 awaits the efforts of its crew to turn it in preparation for its return journey, probably from Peak Forest. This table was put in for the Northwich hopper programme in the mid 1930s. Surely by this time the LMS authorities ought to have realized that a vacuum table was a necessity not a luxury. The crews had some rough times with this turntable and were often helped round by only too willing engine spotters. It was not uncommon for the table to become stuck halfway round, and the bank engine sent for from Tunstead so that assistance could be given by its crew.

Photo H Townley

The hopper train engine crew take the strain as they try to get the table moving with a loco weighing 120 tons. Wooden foot grips have been placed on boarding around the edge of the table since the last picture was taken. Heavy work for an old driver and a young fireman.

Photo J Wooliscroft

Great Rocks June 30th 1950. The 8F for the next set of hoppers is turned ready and stands at the exit signal, whilst 3F 0-6-0 43562, its assisting loco has filled up with water and is setting back to couple up to the 8F for the trip to Tunstead. The pair will remain coupled until reaching Peak Forest North, as the assisting was at this time done from the front. 43562 did quite a long spell at Buxton, being transferred to Crewe South depot in July 1953. A short spell at Gorton in 1959, followed by a return to Buxton in February 1959 where it remained until its withdrawal. As 3562 this loco was involved in a very serious accident at Ashchurch on January 29th 1929.The driver of an express from Bristol to Leeds over ran signals in fog approaching Ashchurch Jct., and crashed into the goods train at 50mph. which was setting back over the trailing crossover from the up to the down propelled by 3562. The pile up was colossal, but luckily, if one can say that, only 4 lives were lost.

Photo H Townley

Newly out shopped 8F 48441 is turned and watered ready for its return to Northwich with the hoppers. The cab side "star" has not yet appeared on this loco. This denoted that the balancing had been modified to allow speeds up to 60 mph to be run. Quite a lot of the class were so treated, but in my own experience, with or without "stars" they all ran as fast as one or another in daily service. Some of the locos were so dirty one could not read the number let alone see the "star".

Photo L.M. Hobdey

A clean 45636 "Uganda" dashes through with an up Manchester – Nottingham express in the summer of 1959. After the introduction of diesels, the long time depot allocations were broken up and these locos found themselves all over the system. 45636 was moved to Leicester, and soon moved to other depots, finally finishing up at Burton depot from where it was withdrawn on December 7th 1962.

Photo L M Hobdey

A very unusual occurrence was the use of an Edge Hill Liverpool Patriot 4-6-0 on a St Pancras to Manchester express in 1960. Luckily caught on camera by Len Hobdey. Obviously something had gone wrong en-route to the booked motive power. 45518 "Bradshaw" climbs the last mile of the gradient towards Peak Forest.

Right at the end of its career 41157 one of the last few compounds still in service, passes on an up slow train in 1959. Once a regular sight on slow trains, compounds were by this time quite a rarity, 41157 soldiered on until withdrawn in May 1960. The Heaton Mersey 4F 44261 stands turned ready to work the evening Peak Forest to Cheadle goods.

Photo J Wooliscroft

Buxton depots 44339 assists the 7/00pm hoppers towards Peak Forest. A task this loco did for years. It is fitted with a coal cover for when it was on snow plough duties which it shared with LNW 0-8-0 49210.

Photo L M Hobdey

Even though class 7 power was available at Kentish Town depot the ever reliable 5MT 4-6-0 was still expected to fill in for absent larger passenger locos. 45407 rushes through with the up "Palatine" express in the summer of 1959. The loco will have worked the down service from St Pancras in the morning, clocking up a respectful 400 miles of far from easy express working. *Photo L M Hobdey*

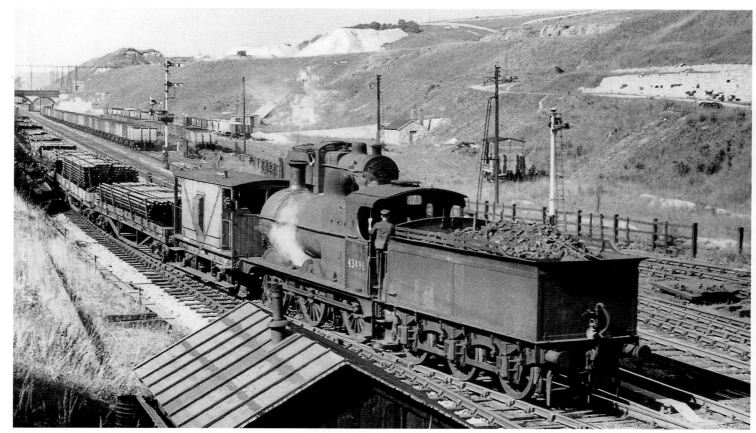

3F 0-6-0 43496 fulfils a Rowsley depot banking turn to Peak Forest. The train of bogie bolster wagons loaded with rails is being put on to the down goods line to Peak Forest out of the way of an express or slow train. *Photo L M Hobdey*

A Saltley depot 9F 2-10-0 92155 passes under Buxton bridge with a train of empty petrol tankers for Stanlow oil refinery. Even when this picture was taken in 1960, the countrys ever increasing use of petrol made these trains a regular sight. The 9F was an ideal loco for this work and a necessary one as larger and heavier tanks were introduced. Carrying class 4 lights, wagons permitting, a maximum speed of 55mph was allowed, with not less than 90% of the train fitted with the vacuum brake.

Photo L M Hobdey

The Northwich fireman is just putting his last round on before reaching the summit, where the dampers will be closed for the long decent to Cheadle Heath. Buxton has provided a newly out shopped 8F 48421 for the banker turn on this day in 1958. No doubt the train engine crew will notice the difference in the amount of help they are receiving from the rear.

Photo L M Hobdey

Hopper train engine and banker leave Great Rocks en-route for Tunstead sidings to work the next down hopper train. The train engine 48683 a regular loco on these turns for years . The banker one of Buxton's LNW 0-8-0s 49057, recently and for the last time new out of the works. The date will be about 1953, as 49057 was withdrawn in May 1957. The loco had been associated with Buxton depot for many years. It was the first LNW tender loco at the depot with its number on the tender in 1923, just after being rebuilt to class G1 from its 3cyl compound form. altered again to class G2a in May 1940. *Photo Author's collection*

Looking south, in 1960, from Buxton bridge over the roof of Great Rocks signal-box. 8F 48654, a Rowsley loco, is signalled for the down goods line with its mixed goods. Banked in the rear by a 2-6-4T which is passing under one of the many over bridges removed in the last 40 years.
Photo L M Hobdey

The last up set of empty ICI hoppers have been accepted by the shunter, who will be waiting at the "dogs home", the name given to the ICI shunter's cabin. Quite often occupied by some soul who had caused trouble, hence the name. The Great Rocks signalman watches the wagons as they pass his box. In the sidings a few "conflat" wagons stand. Whilst in the down lay by a train of vans await their turn for loading. When train loads of vans arrived it was usually the sign that a shipment of hydrated lime was to be made to India. When loaded, the vans, usually three train loads of 40 were taken to Birkenhead docks. I was lucky to be on this job one week and with driver Tom Robinson we went down onto the "float" on the dockside with our train. The vessel "Star of India" was awaiting loading with the contents of 120 vans brought from Tunstead. Another memory of these trips was having to go to ask rather a large policeman, who controlled the crossing at Brook St. if we could pass over with our train We were under the rules of the Docks and Harbour board at this point. The buildings in the background, known as South Shops were the main ICI workshops and maintenance area for locos and road vehicles. *Photo L M Hobdey*

The 7/pm hoppers approach the signal-box with 48045 on the front and 4F 44339 pushing in the rear. 48045 was allocated to Northwich depot for years and served on these jobs with regularity.
Photo L M Hobdey

A view from behind the box shows 70042 "Lord Roberts" at the head of a down express in 1958. The loco, nearly reaching the end of the climb shows it has steam to spare. As previously stated, these locos had complete mastery over these jobs, and could have coped well with a speeding up of the schedule.
Photo L M Hobdey

Great Rocks 2013. Two views of a departing Tunstead to Brent hopper train. The upper shot shows train engine 66706 approaching the now flat roofed signal-box, so altered after a fire burned the original roof. Behind is the "new look" South Shops buildings, a new office block adjacent to the old workshop buildings. On the northern side of the bridge the train engine approaches Peak Forest South, whilst the rear end of the train is still passing Great Rocks. On the extreme right of the picture can just be seen the water filled turntable pit.

Photos Chris Bentley

An EWS class 60 loco 60010 arrives off the single line from Buxton with the Briggs Tunstead hopper empties in 2013. The signalman takes the token from the driver. The single line is worked under the electric token system. The train is then drawn up the goods line, towards Peak Forest, the loco uncoupled to run round the wagons and re-couple at the Great Rocks end before taking the train into Tunstead for reloading. Even though the track formation is as it was years ago, the junction is now the convergence of two single lines, the one from Buxton on the left, the one on the right from Tunstead.

Photos Chris Bentley

Great Rocks August 8th 1964. 4F 0-6-0 44214 assists 8F 2-8-0 48627 on the Corby-Glazebrook ironstone train, and assisted in the rear by a 2-6-4T. It always amazes me that a train like this, made up with dedicated wagons, should have been allowed to continue in service without being fitted with the vacuum brake. 44214 is employed to assist the 8F with the braking of this heavy train down the bank to Cheadle Heath. Rowsley had to provide not only a banker but an assisting loco as well, three crews plus a guard. The wagons were on this service since before 1939, so there had been plenty of time to take this job in hand.

Photo J M Bentley

A view off the bridge of Rowsley 4F 44602 banking a northbound goods train in 1958. The loco is fitted with one of the built up tenders, some were to be found on passenger locos, the rest on 4F 0-6-0s. They were an improvement over the standard Fowler type, at least the fire irons could be safely stowed away without them being perched on top of the coal.

Photo L M Hobdey

Great Rocks 1958. Two views of the hoppers en-route for Northwich. Each train transporting over 1000 tons of Derbyshire down into Cheshire for soda ash production as well as many more uses. In the upper picture a Warrington Dallam depot 8F 48714 has been borrowed by Northwich depot to cover one of its hopper turns. The lower picture another 8F makes steady progress towards the signal-box, the banker looks as if its doing its share of the work.

Photos L M Hobdey

Great Rocks August 5th 1964. Three views, all taken within a few minutes of each other, from off the signal-box steps, show the mid-day procession of northbound freight trains. 48384 is signalled for the down goods with its train of coal, no doubt awaiting the passage of a down passenger. A little later 48278 of Buxton depot passes with a loose coupled trip from Tunstead to Peak Forest. The first couple of 21 ton hoppers destined for the ICI grinding plant adjacent to Taylor`s bank at Peak Forest. Finally 48062 also a Buxton loco, approaches with the Buxton – Dewsnap sidings goods. After the withdrawal of freight from the LNW Buxton to Stockport line freight services were diverted via Peak Forest, Gowhole and the "old road" to Guide Bridge.

Photos J M Bentley

Great Rocks May 13th 1939. Three of the well known Buxton photographers, Messrs Townley, Morten and Hobdey took advantage of a sunny day to get some photos on the main line at Great Rocks. The first shot was of a double headed up ironstone empties with two of the "big goods" in charge. The leading loco 4285 still sporting its shapely Fowler chimney, the train engine 4122 has been fitted with the Stanier version of this long chimney, definitely not as attractive. The starting signal, with distant for Tunstead, is still sighted on the right of the running roads. The second view, a beautifully clean Buxton 2P 4-4-0 447 heads an up slow passenger, consisting of six bogies with a destination of either Derby or Buxton. The old Midland depot at Buxton had, by the time this photo was taken, been closed a few years, but the standard of cleanliness was maintained at the new combined depot. 447 will be at Buxton for a few more years until the wartime reduction of passenger services cause her to be sent away to a depot in need of extra power. ***Photos, upper H Townley, lower L M Hobdey***

To complete the trio of photographs taken on May 13th 1939 is this one of 5XP 5585 "Hyderabad" in charge of an up express. A regular performer on the Midland lines for most of its life, 5585 first appeared in late 1937, when the lines were cleared for the use of this class. When first built, like most of the class, it started life on the West Coast main lines. Crewe North, Willesden, Carlisle Upperby and Rugby depots all had the loco. In September 1937 5585 was allocated to Derby depot, it moved house on the Midland quite a few times, but finished up back at Derby from where it was withdrawn in January 1963.

Photo H Townley

Great Rocks August 1938. An unfortunate derailment of an up fitted goods, caused a considerable mess and no small amount of relaying. Generally speaking the railroad was kept in very good condition and this line was no exception. The 10 foot wheelbase wagons used on these fast jobs were really far from suitable for speeds above 45-55 mph and tended to "nose" from side to side and their ride over junctions could cause much apprehension to crews if one was foolish enough to look back. Luckily in this case nothing was passing on the down road. A 2P 4-4-0 sits on the Buxton breakdown van in the ICI lay-by.

Photos E R Morten

Great Rocks October 7th 1951. An unusual visitor to the Midland lines is seen in the shape and form of 45617 "Mauritius" heading an up special train. At this time 45617 was a Longsight loco, being allocated there from August 1950 until December 1952, when it was transferred to Crewe. The plate laying staff stand well back while the loco makes steady progress over the site of work . The up main is being dug out prior to relaying, note all by hand. The up starting signal, plus distant for Tunstead, is now on the left of the running line and is of the newer upper quadrant type. 8F 2-8-0 48389 itsself a Longsight allocated loco, stands on the down grade side of its spoil train. The first vehicle is an engineers department riding brake, which will be acting as a mess van, the smoke from the chimney denoting that the kettle will be boiling ready for the staff to take their break.

Photos H Townley

Photo H Townley

Great Rocks February 14th 1953. 2-6-4T 42342 passes on the mid-day Chinley to Derby slow train, a job it will do very comfortably indeed. The only drawback would be water capacity. A tender loco on this job would be able to run throughout on one tank of water, whereas 42342 will probably have to top up en-route. 42342 was one of the class members which moved about frequently. At Bournville depot in August 1950, thence to Kirkby in September 1950, Saltley October 1951, Derby March 1952, Nottingham April 1955, Neasden May 1958 and finally Kentish Town in November 1958, where it remained until the end of the decade. The records for this loco must have graced the internal mail system on many occasions whilst en-route from one depot to another.

DRIVER'S REPORT

BRITISH RAILWAYS

Entered on Statement w.e. 12/9/59.

B.R. 32841

Depot. ...Derby... M.P. Area ...Midland... 2 Sept. 1959.

10.45 a.m. A Train from ...Manchester... to ...Dover...

Load (Reg) 15 Bogies Train Loco. No. 44822 Class. ...S.T...

(Act.)

Driver. R. Thompson Fireman. W. Evans Guard.

Depot. Derby Depot. Derby Station.

Reg. No. 321 Reg. No. 321 S.4.8. Weather.

SUBJECT 10/45 "A" Manchester to Dover.

Driver Reports:- 12 Minutes lost due to engine slipping. Disley & Dove Holes Tunnels. Water should have been obtained at Rowsley but there was no supply so I had to make a special stop at Matlock. Both this Water supply is very slow & it took 15 minutes to get 1500 gallons, just sufficient to get the train to Wellingham its next stopping place.

Driver's Signature. R. Thompson
Fireman. 321

Cas.44822. LB.
4.9.59. Derby

A.H. Madden, Esq., LTO(MP), Derby.

G.J. North, Esq., D.M.P.S., Kentish Town.

Copy - C.M & E.E, Room 13, Nelson St., Derby.

10/45 'A' Manchester - Dover.
Engine No.44822. 25.6.59.

The delay to the above train was caused by the engine slipping in Disley and Dove Holes Tunnels (the sands in working order) and due to no water being obtainable at Rowsley necessitating stopping at Matlock Bath where the water was running very slowly.

Will you please therefore cancel the casualty report.

A suitable entry will be made on my casualty statement.

For W. BRAMLEY.

British Railways

LOCOMOTIVE CASUALTY REPORT (MECHANICAL)

B.R. 87315

Locomotive Number 44822
Date Initiated 3. 7. 59

Motive Power ~~West of England~~ Depot KENTISH TOWN District KENTISH TOWN
Date of Casualty 25. 6. 59 Stationed at. DOVER

Locomotive No. 44822 Class 5 MT Allocated to 14B

Driver ___ (No.) Fireman ___ (No.)

Working the 10/45 m Class 'A' Train from MANCHESTER to DOVER
on Sat day, the 25th day of June, 1959.

Assisting [Locomotive No. ___ (No.) Class ___ Allocated to ___]

Assisted by [Driver ___ (No.) Fireman ___ (No.)] Stationed at ___

became a casualty at en route causing a delay of 30 mins. Locomotive changed at ___

No. and Class of Locomotive working forward ___ Regulation Load for locomotive ___ Load of train. ___

NATURE OF CASUALTY TRAFFORD PARK TO STATE, No relevant report at 14B

CAUSE OF CASUALTY (Full description) DERBY
TRAFFORD PARK TO STATE

-do-

PARTICULARS OF REPAIRS CARRIED OUT NECESSITATED BY CASUALTY

-do-

HISTORY OF LOCOMOTIVE NO. 44822

Date and classification of last Shop Repair when the part affected received attention 25.10.58 at Crewe Works L.General

Estimated mileage since 41,400

*Date of last "X" Examination 29. 5. 59 at KENTISH TOWN Depot

Working days since 12

*Date of last Washout. 29. 5. 59 Working days since 12

*Date of last [Daily / Weekly] Examination TRAFFORD PARK TO DAY.
by ___ (No.) Grade. ___

*Date of last Periodical or Mileage Examination 29. 5. 59 Item No. X at KENTISH TOWN Depot
Water test

Estimated period since ___ Extent overdue 12 days

Estimated mileage ___ by ___ (No.) Grade. ___

Date defective part last examined or renewed ___

*If relevant.

Great Rocks October 1st 1955. 5MT 4-6-0 44822 heads an up express past the ICI complex at South Shops. This loco was a long time inmate of Kentish Town depot, in fact it never moved away between 1950 and 1960. Shown with the picture is some of the paper work associated with an incident, which occurred whilst the loco was working the 10/45pm Manchester Central to Dover car sleeper train on Saturday June 25th 1959. This working not shown in the working timetable, ran two nights from Manchester and three nights from Newcastle to Dover utilizing the same stock. Its usual formation was 1 BSO, 4 sleeping cars and 12 bogie CCTS vehicles for the motor cars, a 17 coach train. On the night concerned 44822 backed up on a slightly smaller train of 15 vehicles, a considerable load for a single 5MT loco over Peak Forest. As the attached report shows, 44822 was in very good order, having amassed over 41000 miles since its last general overhaul at Crewe in late 1958. How ever good the loco, a great deal of hard work lay ahead to keep class "A" timings. Trouble started in Disley tunnel, where even with sanders working, 44822 slipped very badly. Things did not look well as might well be expected. Whether or not through Dove Holes tunnel, time was lost as might well be expected. Whether or not the passengers got any sleep during these slipping bouts is doubtful. Once over the top at Peak Forest, 44822 would run fast to Rowsley, where a water stop was booked, as the train was routed to by pass Derby via Chaddesden and rejoin the main line south

of Derby. At Rowsley bad luck stuck again, the water supply was turned off and 44822 would, after the run it had had, need water badly, so a special stop had to be made at Matlock Bath where the water supply was so poor that it took 15 minutes to get 1500 gallons. The driver judged he had sufficient to get him to Nottingham, the next booked stopping point. Opposite is just a little of the paper work generated by the incident. In true railway style, thrown from one department to another until it finally stuck. The loco was well overloaded for the Manchester to Peak Forest section for class "A" timings, yet in none of the reports is the tonnage of the train even mentioned. Taking into consideration the weight of a bogie CCT car carrier, perhaps with 3 cars inside, would be slightly less than a bogie coach and passengers, the 4 sleeping cars would make up for that. A rough estimate of the weight would be 400 tons. Even the driver, who must have had his hands full on this run, just states 15 bogies in his report no weight. The fireman would no doubt be very pleased to see Peak Forest North signal-box go by. Eventually, officialdom decided that slipping in the tunnels and water problems were to blame, not train weight. A total of 8 letters were sent from one department to another over this matter, possibly more not saved, such as why was the water shut off at Rowsley and why was this fact not in the late notice cases at the depots involved. Many thanks to Eric Ellis for providing this information.

45

5XP 4-6-0 5640 "Frobisher" climbs towards Great Rocks with a down express in the very early days of the "red" ones over Peak Forest. 5640 first came to the Midland lines when it was allocated to Sheffield Millhouses depot in December 1935 and worked that depots express turns. The class appears to have had clearance to work the main line north of Derby towards Sheffield before being allowed over the Peak. Re-allocated to Kentish Town depot in February 1937, when the class was permitted over all of the Midland lines. The picture is dated 1938. 5640 made two more moves one to Nottingham and then Derby, before moving to Scotland in the exchange of 1952. It was withdrawn in 1964.

Photo L M Hobdey

Great Rocks 1958. Twenty years after 5640 was photographed here, 70004 "William Shakespeare" is now the motive power for a down express. Ousted by electrification on the "Golden Arrow" service 70004 and 70014 came north to Trafford Park to replace the 5XP and Royal Scots on the St Pancras services.

Photo W A Brown

Great Rocks tunnel June 24th 1959. The last days of the 5XP 4-6-0s on the London-Manchester expresses were getting close when this picture was taken. 45615 "Malay States" a Kentish Town loco heads a train of Mark 1 stock. The fireman`s work is nearly completed, just another mile before the summit is reached. *Photo E R Morten*

Following 45615 on June 24th 1959 is one of the far from successful Crossley Co-Bo Diesels D5714. This class can only be described as a waste of tax payers money. A pair of this class were rostered to work the 4/25pm St Pancras – Manchester express for a period, and failed quite often on this turn. The crews would, when the locos shut down, generally after the climb to Millers Dale, go into the engine room and clout some part of its anatomy with a spanner. If this did not remedy the fault, assistance was required. One evening whilst sitting comfortably in Tunstead sidings, waiting to bank the next set of hoppers, the call came to go to Millers Dale with our 8F to assist this train. Luckily the driver was on the road to Manchester Central. So we duly departed, much shovelling taking place to Millers Dale, where we found D5705 and D5714 dead at the head of 10 bogies. After hooking on we were given the "right away". What a dead weight, the load behind the tender must have been 500 tons or more. The 8F got stuck in for all it was worth. Approaching Tunstead sidings, the Northwich hoppers still stood awaiting a banker. Expecting to see the trip engine going behind him we were more than surprised to see an 8F coming towards us tender first on the front of a failed Sulzer diesel. This was the trip engine assisting the 7/35pm ex Manchester Central which had come to a stand still down the bank towards Chapel-en-le Frith. So both Peak Forest locos were in express service. Assisting these services was not an unusual occurrence, thus the diagramming of class 8F 2-8-0s on these jobs. *Photo E R Morten*

A clean class 60 loco 60079 emerges from Great Rocks tunnel into winter sunshine with a train of loaded 100 ton hoppers on March 29th 2014. Quite a contrast between this view and that of 45615 taken some 55 years previously. *Photo Chris Bentley*

Over the past few years there have been quite a few steam specials over this route. Pictured here is the latest trip run on March 15th 2014 behind two clean 5MT 4-6-0s 45231 "Sherwood Forester" leading. The dark background and the lime covered dead grass in the foreground provide contrast for the locos and stock as the train heads for Buxton. The old LNWR livery suits this class of loco very much and the red backed nameplate is just how it should be. Altogether a grand sight.

Photo Chris Bentley

Right: Great Rocks tunnel 1930. Midland 1P 2-4-0 84 has been pressed into freight train service to assist a 4F 0-6-0 with a down train. The pair are seen emerging from the 161 yard tunnel, with no doubt a bank engine in the rear. Make no mistake these little class 1P 2-4-0 locos were strong, but the picture shows only too well the lack of a decent size freight loco to work these heavy trains. Fowler 7F 0-8-0s were not sufficient in number to cover the bulk of the work. This fell on the classes 2, 3 and 4F 0-6-0s. The class 8F 2-8-0 was still a good few years away. ***Photo F Carrier***

Below: Great Rocks tunnel. By the time this picture was taken freight train haulage had altered out of all recognition when comparing the previous picture. Two class 37 diesels haul a 22 hopper train for Northwich in the 1990s, without a banker. In the back ground, the then new cement plant with its tall chimney, dominates the scenery. Built to supply cement for the channel tunnel scheme, this plant and the one at Earles cement works in the Hope valley were kept busy 24 hours per day, seven days a week. Now this plant has been demolished and replaced by another new plant, much more atmospherically friendly located within the old quarry. ***Photo Chris Bentley***

THE GREAT ROCKS-TUNSTEAD INDUSTRIAL SCENE

Probably the first steam loco to be used at Great Rocks was this rather old and small dummy shaft driven 0-4-0 "Perseverance" hired from Isaac Watt Boulton at Ashton, in 1863-64. The loco worked at Great Rocks quarry until May 1867, when it was returned to Ashton. "Perseverance" was built by Thomas Wheatley in 1858 and was sold to Boulton in 1863. Its main frame was 4 inch thick wood. Just how it performed is not now known. Whether or not it was the loco or the crew who needed perseverance is not recorded. What replaced it at Great Rocks quarry is not known. There is no record of any more of Boultons relics coming this way. A further loco "Dreadnought", an 0-4-0ST with outside cylinders arrived new from the Hunslet Engineering works in 1879 and, in company with an 0-6-0ST purchased from a contractor named Smith in Bury, a Manning Wardle inside cylinder model, did what work was necessary. A Manning Wardle 0-6-0ST their works number 1744 built in 1909 named "Michael" worked at Great Rocks until its sale to the Clay Cross company for their Grin quarry system. Another loco, which became RS 2 under the ICI. and named "Greaseborough" was purchased from the Greaseborough Coal Company at Masborough Rotherham around 1909. This loco was Manning Wardle Works number 1240 built in 1894.

The next acquisition was a loco built for the Clay Cross Company by Avonside Engineering in 1919 their works number1843. This loco may well have been exchanged for the 0-6-0ST "Michael" which went to Grin Quarry from Great Rocks. The arrival of 1919 later renumbered RS 4 started an association with the Avonside type tank loco which lasted to the end of steam working. The 0-6-0ST RS 1 came new from Avonside in 1921 and was the only 6 coupled loco at the end of steam.

In 1923, there must have been a loco shortage at Great Rocks as two of the rather unusual Borrows well tanks built by that firm in St Helens were transferred from Lostock Works Northwich "James Watt" and "Davy" worked until withdrawal in 1933, which probably coincided with the closure of Great Rocks quarry.

The B L F loco stud increased, and further Avonside locos were purchased RS 5, 8, 15 and 16 arrived in 1923-24. Two of the stock were at Hindlow. RS 8 was rebuilt by Harry Townley into a diesel hydraulic and is preserved.

A further second hand purchase was made by the ICI. This was from the firm of Constables at Matlock and was a Manning Wardle 0-4-0ST their works number 1810 of 1913 becoming RS 5. Records show, just to complicate matters that this loco was previously purchased by Constables from the Buxton Lime Firms!

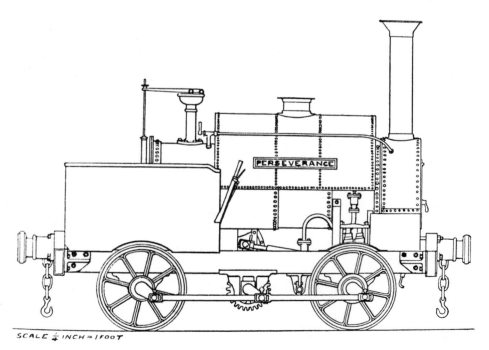

PERSEVERANCE

SCALE ¼ INCH = 1 FOOT

No photographs are known to exist of "Perseverance" but luckily a drawing was done by Alfred Rosling-Bennett for his book The Chronicals of Boultons Sidings. This book first published in 1927, details the happenings at Boultons Works in Ashton. Luckily quite a few pictures were taken of the products of the firm. Isaac Watt Boulton had some influence with the railway companies. He was able to drive his own locomotives around the system. He delivered this contraption to Great Rocks in person. One can only imagine what the trip through Dove Holes tunnel was like. This must have taken place just after the opening of the line.

No pictures have been found of either of the Borrows well tank locos in action at Great Rocks. The picture shown here is of "James Watt" at Lostock Works Northwich before being transferred to Great Rocks in 1923.

The Manning Wardle 0-6-0ST "Michael" built in 1909, their works No 1744 is here seen after its departure from Great Rocks and in the ownership of the Clay Cross company, and working at their Grin Quarry at Ladmanlow. From the dates it looks likely that this loco was exchanged for the Avonside 0-4-0ST which became RS 4.   *Photo Author's collection*

RS 4 is posed for the ICI photographer just after an overhaul and repaint. Originally built for the Grin Quarry Co at Ladmanlow, the loco was purchased or exchanged by the ICI in 1922. It was built by Avonside Engineering of Bristol in 1919. Its building date carried as a numberplate on the tank side. Altogether a neat and useful loco and obviously popular with the quarry owners as they purchased quite a few from the same stable.
Photo La Farge / Tarmac

As work progressed on the new quarry during the 1930s the internal locos were kept very busy indeed. The ICI photographer has had the foresight to chalk the date of his picture on some boards in the foreground November 3rd 1930. The new crossing has been laid across the main line. Why it was ever put in I do not know, for it was never used in normal service. Any departures south were usually drawn up into the cutting, towards the tunnel and used the crossover in front of the signal-box. RS 8 another product of Avonside Engineering is seen busy with the great quarry enlargement, which took most of the 1930s to complete. The whole of the hillside on the right of the picture was removed before the new crusher could be built.
Photo La Farge / Tarmac

After considerable blasting the new cutting linking the old and new workings was completed. This cutting has now been made very much wider and is used by main line locos. Originally only the left hand roads were used by the class 8Fs on arrival with the hoppers, and after being uncoupled had to proceed back the way they had come in to Great Rocks. Now this is all changed as later photographs will show. RS 16 breaks the tape on the occasion of the official opening 11th May 1934. *Photo La Farge / Tarmac*

A later day view of RS 16 involved in shunting duties in the 1950s. She was slightly larger and more bulky than RS 4 and RS 8. A sister loco, RS 15 was to be found at Hindlow works. A total of 5 Avonside locos and 1 Manning Wardle loco plus numerous Simplex petrol locos were the back bone of the ICI stock up until the introduction of diesel locos. *Photo La Farge / Tarmac*

Tunstead sidings February 24th 1954. The only six coupled loco at Tunstead was RS 1, built in 1921 by Avonside, seen here on shunting duties in the cutting. This loco was fitted with a vacuum ejector, as were some of the others including RS 16 so they could draw the 16 bogie hoppers trough the loading bays under the crusher. As all the sidings were on a similar down gradient as the adjacent main line, power was not required to carry out these duties, only brakes. A very useful and convenient situation for the ICI. **Photo Coltas Trust**

RS 1 with driver Len Ashton draws the hoppers through the loading bays. Different grades of stone were loaded in the various bays. When a train was being formed of differing stone sizes part of the train would be gravitated through by the shunter and coupled up to the rear of the first portion. The whole train would then proceed over the weigh bridge and down into which ever sidings road it was to depart from. **Photo La Farge / Tarmac**

Tunstead sidings February 24th 1954. The only exception to the Avonside rule was this Manning Wardle 0-4-0ST RS 5. This loco spent a great deal of time at Peak Dale shunting and propelling wagons of waste up the zig zag to the top of the Great Rocks tip. The lower picture shows the loco awaiting the attention of the scrap man after diesels had taken over the shunting operations. Behind it stands one of the rail mounted steam cranes also awaiting scrapping.

Photos, top Coltas Trust, lower H Townley

South Shops September 30th 1960. RS 16 stands out if service possibly awaiting scrapping. Luckily this did not take place. The loco was purchased privately and went to the Yorkshire Dales railway at Embsay. From there RS 16 went abroad to Belgium. The lower picture shows it at work, looking somewhat small against the European coach at Eeklo Belgium on July 28th 1991. Looking quite smart and carrying the name "Fred" The vacuum brake equipment fitted by the I C I has been removed.   ***Photos top H Townley, lower Manchester Loco Society***

Harry Townley's greatest engineering feat was the conversion of the coal fired kilns at Tunstead to work off natural gas. This was a world first. On the occasion of the official start up Harry, long since retired, came to press the button. The old kilns put about 20 tons of coal dust into the atmosphere every day. With the new kilns all that was stopped, and that great bank of black smoke was not seen again. To mark the occasion one of the Sentinel shunting locos was named in his honour. He stands flanked by Messrs Burton and Goddard, by this time Harry had just about lost his sight.

Photo La Farge / Tarmac

As the end of the 1950s approached, the ICI was looking to replace its stock of steam locos. They were all of the 1920s era and wearing out fast. The various closures of works, and the combining of the Lime and Mond divisions made some diesel locos redundant, and available for transfer. The first diesel loco to work in Tunstead was in fact a South Shops rebuild of an Avonside 0-4-0ST RS 8. Harry Townley their chief development engineer over saw this rebuilding. RS 8 in its new form, not anywhere as pleasant to look at as the steam loco it replaced, was a most useful and handy loco to drive. The position of the cab high up gave the driver a commanding view over all that was happening on the ground. The loco could be driven from all four corners of the cab and its handling was superb. The picture shows it at the Dinting Railway Centre, where it found a home after the ICI had finished with it.

Photo T J Edgington

Left: The first of the "Yorkshire Horses" arrived from down in Cheshire in 1958. Photographed in Tunstead on November 12th of that year. The name "Wallace Ackers" had been bestowed upon it by its previous ICI works. The next of this type "Ludwig Mond" appeared a little later. Various other diesels arrived from works which were closing down. A six coupled loco named "Trevithick" appeared from the works at Settle.

Photo H Townley

The popular "Sentinel" diesel shunters, both the coupled and uncoupled varieties are now very much in evidence. In the upper right picture "Nidderdale" loads the roadstone hoppers from under the new silo. These trains of twelve hoppers ran to destinations in the Manchester area at the time the motorways were being constructed. Their principle destinations being Dean Lane and Collyhurst St., Miles Platting. Originally three train per day to each destination, hauled by class 25 locos. It is fair to say they ran like clockwork. The lower picture shows another of the type in more recent days when the firm was known as "Buxton Lime Industries". Named after the Peak District beauty spot "Dovedale".

Photos Top Right: La Farge / Tarmac
Lower: Chris Bentley

Tunstead December 5th 1930. The LMS authorities opened the new signal-box at Tunstead on October 26th 1930. Their contribution towards this massive enterprise, meant that most of the stone removed from the the hillside which stood in the way of building the crusher and associated siding, could now be loaded into trains and taken away. Also materials required for building purposes could arrive by this new route. The cutting linking Great Rocks with the new site was not yet finished. A Buxton 3F 0-6-0 3282 stands awaiting the road with a train of stone. A group of officials examine the new point work recently installed. *Photo La Farge / Tarmac*

A view off the quarry floor shows much work in progress. The site for the new kilns is itsself a quarry, complete with narrow gauge tracks, for the removal of stone after blasting. New temporary tracks have been laid to join up with the main line exit. A train of loaded wagons of stone stands on what was to become the main departure road adjacent to the down main line. A 4F propels its train of empty wagons across the road in front of the signal-box before bringing them into the site for loading *Photo La Farge / Tarmac*

Tunstead Sidings October 4th 1937. The years of planning by the ICI for this new quarry, crusher and sidings, was by this date beginning to come into fruition. The new bogie hoppers, built by Chas. Roberts, were being delivered and the idea of running block trains to Northwich became a reality. Starting in a small way, with a 4F 0-6-0 and eleven hoppers, assisted in front by another 4F to Peak Forest the trains became part of the timetable. The ICI photographer took this posed picture, it shows that the original arrival and departure road is still intact in the foreground.

Photo La Farge / Tarmac

Tunstead Sidings December 1st 1938. Just over 12 months later, 8F 2-8-0 8026, stands awaiting departure with the new load of 17 hoppers, the assisting loco a 4F will be in front. The temporary departure roads have been removed and the site is settling down to the purpose it was designed for, the mass movement of stone into Cheshire. The second world war was not far away, and Harry Townley once told me how glad the ICI was that this venture was in full production before the war started.

Photo La Farge / Tarmac

An Freightliner class 66 loco 66601 heads towards Great Rocks after leaving a train of bogie cement tanks under the loading silo. A great deal of tidying up has been done in this area. The buildings do not have the thick coat of lime dust anymore, fences divide the road system from the rail side of the business. The complete lack of pollution can be seen, compare this picture with the earlier ones where the coal fired kilns blackened the sky every day of the year and the lime dust in the atmosphere made ones eyes water and skin burn.

Photo Chris Bentley

Tunstead Sidings 2012. The original cutting, now very much wider and laid with main line standard track throughout, where as in the old days only part of the layout was able to take main line locos, the rest being laid with much lighter industrial track. A class 66 loco has arrived with a train and is about make its way back to Great Rocks.

Photo Chris Bentley

Tunstead Sidings 2012. A class 60 loco looking very smart in its red livery, departs the sidings with a train load of 100 ton hoppers. Above it, on the bank side is that wonderful dry stone wall, built in 1864, at the time of the building of the line, looking remarkably neat. A tribute to the men who built things to last.

Photo Chris Bentley

Above: Buxton depots 42368 exits Great Rocks tunnel with the teatime Chinley – Buxton train on August 18th 1951. The photographer Ray Morten is stood on the long since demolished over bridge.

Bottom Left: Whilst waiting to cross over and go into the sidings with the banking loco, a down goods approached. I had just time to get the camera out to obtain this shot of 70043 "Lord Kitchener" as it passed with a heavy down goods, banked in rear by a 2-6-4T.
Photo J M Bentley

Bottom Right: 48744 passes the box at Tunstead with a Gowhole Siding to Chaddesden special freight on April 23rd 1966. The loco and crew should have been working the Buxton-Chaddesden freight turn, but this being cancelled they were sent to Gowhole to work this train instead. This would effect their finishing time some what. *Photo J M Bentley*

Left: Taken from the footplate of the class 8F on the banker turn, stood on the up main line whilst the trip loco 44364 lifts a heavy train out of the sidings for Peak Forest, where all the individual loads will be sorted for their various destinations. The loco, having been transferred to Buxton from Bletchley, was in very good order having had an easier life than our 4Fs. Fitted like quite a lot of the class with an exhaust injector, the steam supply for this coming from the pipe at the base of the smoke-box, along under the foot frame, via the grease separator, from which steam can be seen blowing to the injector under the footplate step. The only problem with the exhaust injector was its inability to pick up water whilst working heavily at slow speeds as 44364 is doing here. The loco subsequently sheared a trailing crank pin whilst trying to pull back a train which had been unable to stop at Buxton East Jct. signals. 44364 finished its days as a stationary boiler at Gorton depot.

Photo J M Bentley

Below: Northwich 8F 2-8-0 48045 gives all its got lifting the down loaded hoppers out of the sidings in the 1950s on what appears to be a greasy rail. Behind no doubt will be 44339. After the commencement of the running of this service the load was reduced from 17 loaded hoppers to 16.

Photo Author's collection

Tunstead December 1st 1938. The original departure roads are clearly seen in this picture, and the original method of assistance, a 4F in front. The lime sidings, as roads 1 to 4 were known remained pretty much unaltered. The problem for the two locos on the front was slipping, not an easy job to get the 17 hoppers moving. Frequent coupling breakages occured.

Photo La Farge / Tarmac

A Johnson 4-4-0 2425, passes where Tunstead will appear many years after the date of this photograph, which is circa 1901. The bridge over which the loco passes carried the line over what was once a river, long since dried up or gone underground. The loco carries what was then the Midland express head lamp code, top and left, this altered a couple of years later when the Railway Clearing House instructed the companies to adopt a standard express headlamp code of one lamp on each buffer. The Somerset and Dorset railway never adopted this lamp code where this lamp code top and left remained until the end of the line

Photo Author's collection

About 27 years later than the previous picture, an LMS 3cyl compound passes the same site with an 8 coach down express. The loco 1059, one of the early batch of LMS builds with the drivers position on the right of the cab, looks little troubled by its load as it heads up the 1 in 90 gradient towards Great Rocks tunnel.

Photo Author's collection

A heavy loose coupled train of 25 ton hopper wagons and cov-hops leaves for Runcorn behind an 8F with a 4F banker. Whilst on the down main a "Crab" 2-6-0 approaches with a goods, which will have to clear Great Rocks before the 8F gets the road out on to the main line. Behind the 8F is the ICI engine shed and water tower.
Photo La Farge / Tarmac

The last days of the old bogie hoppers was approaching when this picture was taken. Two 37 class locos start a train of 22 hoppers en-route for Northwich. To prevent coupling breakages on these heavy trains the hoppers have by now been fitted with "instanter" three link couplings. In the background are some of the new air brake hoppers, which are now the normal vehicles for these trains. Alterations have been made to the lime roads, single wagon loads are no longer dealt with, traffic is now in block trains. The old main line on the left of the picturenow looks more like a sidings road itself. The photograph taken from off the top of the causeway linking the old quarry with the new quarry on "Old Moor"
Photo La Farge / Tarmac

Two final views over the north end of the sidings and works. In the upper picture the tunnel under the causeway can be seen in the distance. In the ICI cutting a train of empty hoppers waits to be drawn down and loaded. On the next road are the air brake covered wagons used for the lime train to Margam South Wales. The lower picture shows the crusher and its associated conveyor belts and the final extent of the old quarry face. Even in the mid 1990s when these pictures were taken the old quarry was finished with and tipping was beginning to fill the quarry floor. One of the Sentinel diesels is drawing a train under the silos for loading. The slip road in the foreground allowed access into the sidings for the arriving hopper engines, and a release road for locos heading for Buxton via the single line to Great Rocks.

Photos Chris Bentley

A view taken off the quarry floor looking south shows some very full lime roads. The Middlewich train stands on No 5 road, 6&7 roads stand empty awaiting the arrival of loaded hoppers. The ICI wagon repair staff will shut the road after the hoppers are position, whilst they carry out their examination and re-blocking if required. In the far distance, a line of wagons can be seen in the sidings at Peak Forest Jct. This siding was on an ash tip and did what ash tips do well, it started to smoulder and eventually had to be abandoned. The fire started to threaten the main line, so a large valley was dug out and filled with stone to prevent it spreading any further.

Photos La Farge / Tarmac

The sidings as they are today. The first thing which strikes you is how "mother nature" has taken over. In the previous picture there is hardly a tree in sight, now a forest has appeared, not only on the hillside, but on the edge of the quarry. The sidings have been rationalized, most of the lime roads have gone with the ending of single wagon load traffic. A road has been put in down to what was called "back pastures" to facilitate dumper loading.

Photo Chris Bentley

An up to date picture from the south looking towards the newest tunnel in the Peak, a short length under the causeway which links the old quarry and the Old Moor workings. A train of loaded hoppers stands on No 1 road, a train of empty vehicle is on No 4.

These sidings lines look in far better order than the adjacent single line to Buxton.
*Photo **Chris Bentley***

A Northwich 8F makes its way up to the exit signal with a down loaded hopper train in the late 1950s. The 4th hopper back is passing over the never used south departure crossing, now partly replaced with straight rail. The lower picture taken from the quarry floor shows the banker, a 4F fitted with a tender cab doing its stuff in the rear. A few hoppers and various wagons occupy the cripple road, whilst one of the ICI locos stands at the head of train of 16 ton steel wagons, moving them for loading via the shute from the quarry floor. The wagons took quite a hammering when the stone came down the shute, quite a drop, it certainly caused movement in the wagon springs.

Photos Author's collection

The departure of a train of down hoppers on July 9th 1960. 48340 takes the strain as it starts away from No 6 road The loco, recently out shopped, has the "star" denoting altered balancing to allow higher running speeds. Just to spoil the turn out 48340 has been fitted with a Fowler 3500 gallon tender. The concrete dome on the right of the picture is one of the blasting shelters provided by the ICI for the safety of its workers. If a well blast was to take place at the south end of the quarry, BR locos had to vacate the sidings and stand up in the cutting by the signal-box *Photo Author's collection*

71

A Rowsley 3F 0-6-0 43342 banks the evening Runcorn train out of Tunstead. That depot had odd banking turns out of Tunstead rostered to fit in with their other banking duties from Rowsley. The 12/20pm Northwich hoppers was such an instance. The load of 16 cov-hops and 25 ton hoppers is unusually small, normally this job loaded up to 29 cov-hops, a much stiffer load for the Heaton Mersey crew to hold back down to Cheadle Heath. In the foreground the old river bed has not yet been levelled off and in the background that wonderful piece of dry stone walling, still as good as the day it was built in 1864. One evening, whilst stood in the sidings during a thunder storm, part of this wall was struck, making the first gap in it for 100 years. *Photo La Farge / Tarmac*

5MT 4-6-0 45220 passes the sidings with a Derby-Manchester slow train. The cabin in the background was the ICI sidings staff mess room. The roof was made of railway sleepers covered in corrugated iron. After a well blast one day, the staff returned to find that a rock had come straight through the roof, it had smashed all the tables and buried its self into the ground underneath the cabin. That is why the ICI was so particular about blasting shelters.

Photo J M Bentley

73

48640 pulls out with the last steam hauled 6pm hoppers on July 31st 1964. Steam engines put in many more appearances on this turn and others because of diesel failures. *Bottom Left:* 48744 is seen at the rear of the hoppers on January 18th 1966 waiting for the guard to finish his duties The train engine is a Sulzer Type 2 diesel. Whilst banking these trains with a 8F, the experience of a very sudden stop, because the driver in front had let his foot slip off the dead mans pedal, was by no means pleasant, especially if the fireman was putting a round on. It was akin to running into a stop block with full steam on. ***Photo J M Bentley***

Bottom Right: March 16th 1961. The only time during my footplate career that I worked a southbound train out of this sidings was on this occasion, when we worked a special of rough stone for Ilkeston.

The motive power was a Rowsley 4F 44602. To get the train out of the sidings and up into the cutting, we required the assistance of the hopper banking loco on the brake van end of the train. ***Photo J M Bentley***

5MT 4-6-0 45075 gives of its best as it passes Tunstead with the Buxton – Dewsnap Sidings freight on April 21st 1966. Heavy freight trains certainly took some moving on this gradient with large wheel locos. The start from Peak Forest Jct., with loco and train on the right Blackwell Mill curve, and the prevailing 1 in 90 gradient could be very difficult. The reverse curves towards Tunstead gave the loco very little chance to get the train on the move. ***Photo J M Bentley***

Buxton depots 8F 48088 passes with a down goods on the same day. The empty tar tanks are on the first leg of their journey back to Ellesmere Port. These tanks plied between there and Hillhead quarry sidings at Harpur Hill for years, supplying the tarmac plant. They, like lots more traffic appeared on the Midland side after the LNW line from Buxton to Stockport was made a passenger only line.

Photo J M Bentley

Taken around 1930, this picture shows a 2F 0-6-0 running light engine back to Rowsley after banking a goods train to Peak Forest. The picture was taken by the ICI photographer to record how it all looked before the Tunstead quarry and associated sidings were built. A cold looking Peak District day. ***Photo La Farge / Tarmac***

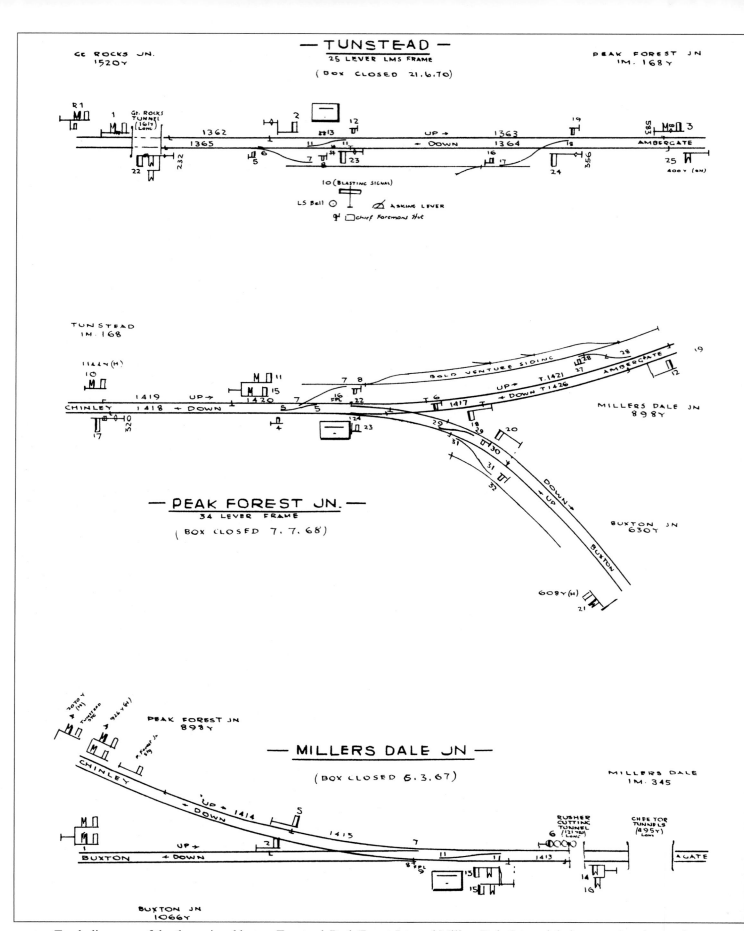

Track diagrams of the three signal boxes, Tunstead, Peak Forest Jct. and Millers Dale Jct. and their respective closure dates.

A Belle Vue depot 3F 3596 heads a single train (a train with no banker required) past Peak Forest Jct. The train, about 20 wagons in length, comprises mainly of coal and will have commenced its journey at Rowsley. For the crew this will be a "day out". The 3F shows that steam is in good supply, as it always was with these locos. They were a joy to fire, the bottom section of the Midland fire hole door up, coal was put into the fire box between it and the top flap, the blast of the loco took the coal off the shovel. All the fireman had to do was point the shovel in the direction he wanted the coal to go. It was always necessary to keep a good fire under the door and in the back corners.

Photo Author's collection

48138 in charge of a down through goods has just passed through the short Peak Forest Jct. tunnel on August 29th 1964. Above the tunnel was the only access in to the ICI Central Works for road vehicles. The quarry was, by this time, closed.

Photo J M Bentley

This picture of 48329, taken off the bank side by the tunnel shows the junction signals for the branch to Buxton. The train looks as if it ought to be running on higher classification lamps than it is with all the wagons fitted with the vacuum brake. With the up distant at caution the driver will be expecting to stop at Millers Dale Jct. The picture was taken by W D Cooper on March 23rd 1963.

On the same day 23rd March 1963, W D Cooper took this rather fine view from ground level of 48297 on an up goods approaching the junction. Not a train which will be causing the loco or crew much trouble. This 8F was built by Beyer Peacock, their works No 7043 in 1941. The loco became War Dept. 449, and went out to Persia. Whilst working there after the war was renumbered 41-241. On return to this country it became 48297. On many of these locos the Persian numerals could be easily seen under the skimpy coat of paint afforded by BR. A little effort with a piece of chalk could easily re-number them. The Peak Forest Jct. down starting signal is on the left of the picture.

Peak Forest Jct. August 1937. 5MT 4-6-0 5036 passes the junction with an up special M 712, possibly running in connection with Bakewell show. The LMS ran literally hundreds of special trains to events far and wide. The new plate layers cabin has just been completed. The LMS was at this time trying to update facilities for its staff. The outbreak of war brought this plan to an abrupt halt. ***Photo H Townley***

Same place and same photographer, but 22 years later. Rebuilt Royal Scot 4-6-0 46142 "The York and Lancaster Regiment" is heading an up express on September 20th 1959. The only difference between the photographs (except the locos) is that flat bottomed track has been laid on the main line in place of the bullhead variety and the plate layers cabin looks a little more weathered, but still in good order. No signs of activity in Central Works, as it had just about finished by then. ***Photo H Townley***

Peak Forest Jct. March 23rd 1963. Fowler 2-6-4T 42379 enters the Blackwell Mill curve en-route to Buxton after working the morning Sheffield passenger turn. During my railway career I often wondered why a concrete signal post was provided for the up branch home signal No 20. Through the good offices of Manchester Loco Society member Trevor Moseley, a retired Signal and Telegraph man, who studies signalling history, all was revealed. He writes -;

The signal itself is something of a rarity being of concrete construction, instead of the more usual pitch pine ones used by the company. Due to the severe timber shortages caused by the effects of the 1st World War, the Midland Railway along with the Great Central and Great Northern railways, purchased concrete signal posts from the Midland & Great Northern Joint Railway. This company were the pioneers in this material for railway engineering applications and had their own concrete works at Melton Constable in Norfolk. One thing that was missing from this signal post however was the ladder staging at the top of the post, something that was standard on all Midland wooden signal posts.

Whilst repairs were being carried out on Blackwell Mill viaduct, the line between Buxton Jct. and Millers Dale Jct. was closed on Sundays. The service from Buxton was diverted via Peak Forest Jct. where it crossed over from the down to the up main line. The picture shows the unit having done that move and is proceeding towards Millers Dale. Even at this late date the ICI have put new tops on the kiln chimneys, although little more was to come out of this quarry The date of this picture taken by Harry Townley was September 20th 1959.

8F 2-8-0 48081 at the head of a down goods approaches the junction on a sunny but cold looking March 23rd 1963. The backdrop of "Little Switzerland" is clearly seen in this photograph, a natural quarry face, not a man made one. 48081 for many years a Kirkby loco, was re-allocated to Rowsley in June 1959.   *Photo W D Cooper*

5MT 4-6-0 45412 follows the train headed by 48081, heading northward towards Peak Forest Jct. assisted in the rear by a Rowsley 2-6-4T. With the exception of the two bogie bolster wagons next to the loco, the train consists of coal. 45412 was a Carlisle allocated loco for the entire 1950s decade, moving to the Liverpool division in May 1960.   *Photo W D Cooper*

Two old views of loading in the cramped lime covered siding at Central Works. The actual loading has progressed from shovels to overhead skips. In later days this area was given an awning so that the loading area was a little more protected from the elements. The wagons are being sheeted as soon as they are loaded. In the lower picture the daily shunting loco has arrived, and empty wagons are being drawn out in readiness for transfer into the quarry sidings. In the foreground are wagons of slack coal awaiting unloading onto the narrow gauge and being propelled up the incline to feed the kilns. *Photos La Farge / Tarmac*

This wonderful panoramic view was taken by the local Buxton photographer Mr Board in the early 1930s from Topley Pike. It shows the arrival of two locos, a 4F and a 3F, both needed to get the loaded wagons out of the sidings and the empty ones in. With this system being on a 1 in 90 gradient, the propelling of wagons down gradient was strictly forbidden, as any break loose would result in a run away down gradient towards Millers Dale with disastrous consequences. One of the locos would be on the down gradient side at all times. The rear portion of what will eventually be their train stands in the lay-by. In the upper left of the picture, the first quarrying is taking place in what was to become Tunstead Sidings. The area above is still green fields and a wood, which will eventually become part of the largest limestone quarry in the world.

Photo Derbyshire County Council / Buxton Museum

Blackwell Mill 1948. One of the early LMS built 4F 0-6-0s 4040 passes the quarry sidings with an up goods. In the quarry the kilns look as if they have just had a round of coal put on. The thick pall of smoke, a regular sight in the Peak District in those days, was long before the environment was considered. Only work for men was the priority then. *Photo H Townley*

Blackwell Mill 1989. The kilns are long gone, all rail activity reduced to a single line to Buxton. The restoration work being carried out by the quarrying industry can be seen to good advantage in this picture. The scene in 2013 is even more dramatic, with most of the quarry filled in and vast numbers of trees planted, there will soon be no sign of its industrial past. Compare the upper left of this picture with the view taken in the 1930s by Mr Board, it shows well the massive expansion that has taken place at Tunstead quarry. *Photo Chris Bentley*

Blackwell Mill March 23rd 1963. A work stained 4F 44286, a Heaton Mersey engine of long standing, heads an up train of empty wagons for Rowsley yard. Running with class 7 lights, express freight, non fitted, with a maximum speed of 40 mph. ***Photo W D Cooper***

After the commencement of the building of the line towards Manchester, the first large construction job was the Wye Valley viaduct. This structure was only a few yards to the north of the then new junction with the Buxton line. Luckily a great amount of stone was removed from the cutting through which 44286 is passing in the previous picture, and this did not have to be transported far to form the viaduct embankment, as this picture shows well. The stone from these cuttings was also the main supply for the miles of dry stone walling on the boundary of the line. The picture was taken from off the Buxton line embankment. ***Photo Author's collection***

Millers Dale Jct. A Newton Heath Austerity 2-8-0 90715 climbs towards Peak Forest with a down goods. An Ivatt 2-6-0 stands at the branch end home signal awaiting a road back to Rowsley after banking a train to Buxton.   *Photo W A Brown*

Millers Dale Jct. May 15th 1948. A Hellifield depot "Austin Seven" 9671 in full cry crosses the junction with a through freight destined for the Brindle Heath yards. 9671 was not to last much longer, being withdrawn from Aintree depot a few years later in March 1952. The withdrawal of these locos came very quickly in the early 1950s, very few were left by the end of the decade.   *Photo H Townley*

On the same day, May 15th, 8712 of Buxton depot, takes the branch towards Buxton with a goods from Rowsley with driver Eric Wilson in charge. This was one of the first of this class to be allocated to Buxton depot just after the war. Most of our early allocations were in the 8700 series. 8712 was at the depot for over 20 years.
Photo H Townley

Two views of down goods trains passing over the Buxton line junction in May 1948. 3F 3370 of Rowsley depot at the front of a through goods, possibly for Trafford Park. 3370 remained at Rowsley until its withdrawal in 1959. 4F 0-6-0 3970 in the same spot on the same day makes her way towards Peak Forest. The 3900 series were reputed to be the best of all this class, 3970 has lost its shapely Fowler chimney in favour of one of the Stanier type. The up main home signal is still sited on the right of the running lines, as in Midland practice, but the home signal off the Buxton branch is on the left of the running line.

Photos W D Cooper

Millers Dale Jct. circa 1932. A Manchester bound express passes the junction hauled by a 3cyl compound 4-4-0 with a 9 coach load. Had this copy of the picture been printed on glossy paper the result would have been a really superb shot, taken from a wonderful vantage point high up above the recently relayed junction. In the foreground is another example of the quality dry stone walling the Midland company commissioned.

Photo Author's collection

A Rowsley "Crab" 2-6-0 2845 hauls a down goods past the junction in May 1948, taken by W D Cooper, who took advantage of the continuous procession of trains, in both up and down directions. It was also a pleasant place to have a picnic. The first wagon is a very much enlarged 21 tonner, its capacity increeased by the fitting of four rows of rails around the top. The days of the steel wagon was fast approaching, soon they would be the rule not the exception.

A long time Rowsley allocated 4F 44134 passes the box with a down through goods. The three junction signal-boxes were very lonely places in which to spend a night shift. This box and Buxton Jct. box had no running water and relied on the afternoon shunter from Buxton to pick up the empty water cans on its way to Millers Dale, and deposit the full ones on its way back. ***Photo E Johnson collection***

A rare visitor to the Midland lines is seen here heading a down express past Millers Dale Jct. 45670 "Howard of Effingham" long time resident of Edge Hill depot Liverpool, obviously borrowed by Trafford Park, in a time of loco shortage. Longsight depot would send a spare 5XP across Manchester to ease matters, but Liverpool locos were not often involved. *Photo W A Brown*

Trafford Park depot's 70021 "Morning Star" passes the junction at speed with an up morning express to London. The crew will be having a much more pleasant ride over this heavily curved line on the Britannia than they would have had on a 4-6-0. *Photo W A Brown*

Above: Rusher Cutting tunnel March 23rd 1963. 92051, one of the Rowsley stud of 9F 2-10-0s enters the tunnel with an up goods. This loco and 92008/9, 92047-50 were allocated to that depot in November 1959. The 1938 accident to a down special passenger train took place at the far end of this tunnel. **Photo W D Cooper**

Right: Whether or not 9F 2-10-0s were allocated to Rowsley depot, its 4F 0-6-0s still carried out a great deal of the freight haulage. One of the allocation, 44556 emerges from the tunnel with a down goods on March 23rd 1963. Looking a little worse for wear, but no doubt still in good mechanical order, as most of the Rowsley allocation usually were. **Photo W D Cooper**

ACCIDENT IN RUSHER CUTTING TUNNEL SUNDAY MAY 2ND 1938

This accident took place at 5.35am on May 2nd. The rail system was that week-end coping with a great number of football specials.

Two northern teams played for the F.A. cup that year. Preston North End and Huddersfield, Preston being the winners by one goal.

Three of the country`s main lines bore the brunt of running these special trains. Euston, St Pancras and Marylebone stations being the main participants.

This particular train had left St Pancras at 1am, loaded with Preston supporters who, no doubt had had a very good night out celebrating their victory.

The amazing thing about this accident is that there appears to be absolutely no official report into its circumstances, even though involved a passenger train in which injuries were sustained. The Board of Trade do not seem to have ordered an enquiry. Only an internal one was held at Millers Dale on Tuesday May 4th.

At the time of writing no sign of this internal report can be found. It was obviously done by the general managers office at Derby and when these offices were cleaned out when they were due for demolition, the report could well have been thrown out.

THE FACTS

A goods train had preceded the special passenger from Rowsley and was put on the down slow line at Lime Sidings, to await the passage of the special train, which it was intended to follow probably as far as Great Rocks, where no doubt it would again be put inside to allow another special cup final train to pass.

The loco on the special train was not in good order and obviously short of steam. The run through Millers Dale had "winded" the loco and the driver decided to stop at Millers Dale Jct. signal-box for a "blow up" There is no record of the class of loco involved, it would more than likely be a 5MT 4-6-0 or a compound 4-4-0.

In accordance with the plan, the goods train drew out of the slow line platform at Millers Dale after the special had cleared the starting signal. The visibility was very poor, with a thick mist enshrouding the valley. The goods train proceeded slowly towards the starting signal.

The exact circumstances of just what happened is not known. The driver of the goods train was obviously happy that he was "right away", but as he accelerated towards Millers Dale Jct. was unaware that the special had stopped short of steam, its rear coaches still inside Rusher Cutting tunnel.

On realizing that the goods train was on its way towards him, the signalman at Millers Dale Jct. George Hayto, ran from his box with a red lamp and detonators, but was unable to get to the rear of the passenger train before the goods train struck the rear coach.

The fireman of the goods train, having just put a round of coal on

was thrown hard against the boiler front and was injured, but never the less set off back to see their guard and to protect the rear of the train.

Inside the passenger train it was obviously chaotic, the rear coach (a steel one) had been lifted off its bogies, and quite a few passengers were injured, luckily nobody was killed. What a place for an accident no roads anywhere near by, no lights, and only the residents of the Blackwell Mill cottages who, when roused, came in force to help the injured and shocked passengers. Most of the passengers were asleep when the accident happened.

Local doctors were summoned from Buxton and Tideswell and the nearest an ambulance could get was Blackwell Mill.

The following Cup Final special was stopped at Millers Dale, where a fleet of buses eventually arrived to take the passengers forward to Buxton, where they were taken by train to Manchester. The rest of the specials were diverted at Ambergate towards Sheffield and the Hope Valley line.

The amazing thing was, after the remains of the rear coach was uncoupled, the rest of the special proceeded on its way to the North West after being examined and pronounced fit to continue. This just left the wreckage of the rear coach, which the breakdown crews had cleared by mid-morning.

What the final verdict was is unknown, and I suppose this is where the speculation starts.

Rusher Cutting tunnel 2014. Two pictures showing the tunnel as it is today. Its title board above the arch instead at the side as it used to be. Rock instability must have worried the engineers when the line was originally being built. Not only was the line put into a short tunnel, but massive buttresses were constructed to prevent any movement, as the tunnel wall was in fact right on the edge of the embankment. When one looks at the size of the blocks used for these buttresses, no chances were being taken with their ability to support what was above. The Victorian engineers certainly made a "belt and bracers" job of this construction as no serious movement has ever taken place.

Photos Steve Allsop

Rusher Cutting May 1959. A Trafford Park Scot 4-6-0 46122 "Royal Ulster Rifleman" traverses the cutting with an up express, when class 7 locos first appeared on these turns. 46122 had been transferred from Longsight to Trafford Park in May 1959, only staying there one month before being transferred away to Carlisle Upperby depot.

Photo W A Brown

LMS 3cyl compound 4-4-0 41157 climbs through the cutting with a down slow passenger train. This loco was one of the last in regular service, along with 40907 at Millhouses depot. 41157 soldiered on until May 1960 when it was withdrawn from Derby depot.

Photo E Johnson collection

Rusher Cutting July 1951. A beautiful view of the cutting in its entirety. The picture shows well how little room the original builders of the line had available. The stone removed for the building of the line had to be tipped carefully down towards the river which flows at the very base of the embankment. The other alternative would have been another expensive tunnel. Class 2P 0-4-4T 41905 heads "wrong line" towards Millers Dale with the service from Buxton, whilst engineering works were taking place on the short viaduct between the Chee Tor tunnels.

Photo E R Morten

A Derby depot 5MT 44839 is the power for the Nottingham – Liverpool express in the mid 1950s. 44839 had moved to Derby depot in September 1953 from Bath, where it had worked on the Somerset & Dorset section. On arrival at Manchester Central another 5MT or even a 2-6-4T will couple to the rear of the train for its express run to Liverpool Central. ***Photo E Johnson collection***

48297 of Speke Jct. depot emerges from Chee Tor tunnel No 2 with a down coal train on March 23rd 1963. Another picture taken by W D Cooper, one of around 12 he took on this occasion whilst rambling around from Blackwell Mill to Chee Dale.

Another down coal train emerges from Chee Tor tunnel No2, this time hauled by a Heaton Mersey 8F 48327. This loco started the 1950s decade at Willesden, moving to Birkenhead in November 1950, thence to Heaton Mersey in September 1953, where it remained until the early 1960s when it moved to Buxton.

Photo Author's collection

Top left: Chee Tor tunnel No2. 2P 0-4-4T 41905 emerges from the 94 yard long tunnel with the up "pull and push" service from Buxton on July 15th 1951. The loco was at this time on loan to Buxton, from Longsight to cover the absence of the Midland 0-4-4T 58083, which was having its last general overhaul at Derby.

Photo E R Morten

Top right: Fowler 2-6-4T 2372 exits Chee Tor tunnel No1 and crosses the short viaduct between the two tunnels with the through St Pancras – Buxton coach. 2372 was at Buxton for just a short while in 1948, this picture being taken in May of that year. Its next depot was Barrow, where it remained until transferred to Stockport Edgeley in October 1959.

Photo W D Cooper

Left: The driving end of the "pull and push" set emerges from Chee Tor No1 tunnel on May 25th 1952.
Photo E R Morten

Another view of the wrong line working on July 1st 1951. 5XP 4-6-0 45626 "Seychelles" passes the site of work, the small viaduct between the two tunnels, with an up express. The brickie's scaffolding can be seen along with the piles of new bricks, off loaded from wagons on to the track side. The loco, a regular on these services still sports a boiler with dome and top feed combined.

Photo E R Morten

Chee Tor tunnel No 1 May 25th 1952. Two views taken from within the tunnel of up passenger trains by Ray Morten. The express, headed by another regular 5XP 4-6-0 45622 "Nyasaland" a Trafford Park allocated loco.

Preceding the express by a few minutes is the up slow passenger, having picked up any would be passengers at Chapel-en-le-Frith and Peak Forest for London or stations to Derby. The train will stand on platform 2 at Millers Dale whilst the express picks up and puts down passengers wishing to travel to stations to Matlock or Buxton. The train engine is a compound 41143 of Derby depot, recently transferred from Scotland where it had spent most of its working life. It came south in October 1951. Sister locos 40907, 41136 and 41180 also spent their last years south of the border.

The present day scene. The tunnels now lit so that walkers and cyclists can see where they are going. Despite its popularity as a walk way, this still ought to be an operational railway, giving access for the North West into St Pancras.

Photo Chris Bentley

Millers Dale 1951. This fine view to the south of Chee Tor No 1 tunnel shows 41905 propelling its two coach set towards the tunnel. The train is passing the site of East Buxton quarry or Station Quarry as it was known. The train is just on the short East Buxton viaduct, even by this date completely shrouded with trees. Originally a signal-box was provided here in the early days of the line named East Buxton Lime Sidings. The original box being re-framed in 1895, and a replacement box opened on October 11th 1901. The new box closed in June 1933, as quarrying activities lessened. All the required movements were then covered by the station box. The remains of the quarry and the kilns can be seen well in this picture, although taken over 60 years ago. Very little beautification work has been done by man up to this time, but "mother nature" is fast taking over. With the closure of this quarry, shunting work at Millers Dale was greatly reduced. The station yard and warehouse dealing with the requirements of the local coal merchants and farmers.

Photo E R Morten

Two views of trains emerging from Chee Tor No1 tunnel, 401 yards in length on September 1st 1953. 41905 heads the pull and push towards the station. The driver Jack Wood has noticed the photographer. The coal in the bunker is getting down, which denotes the loco is working the middle turn roster, seven trips for both loco and crew. On the same date 48714 a Warrington based loco heads an up train of empty wagons for Rowsley sidings. This picture shows the dry stone wall built above the tunnel entrance as a protection against falling stone from the hill above.

Photos E R Morten

Taken from the window of Millers Dale station signal-box it shows 8F 2-8-0 48250 working an up goods on May 25th 1964. Even though the loco carries through freight lamps, it will only be through as far as Rowsley, where everything had go into the yard to be shunted.

Photo J M Bentley

Millers Dale August 1ˢᵗ 1938. A Buxton 2P 4-4-0 461 runs into the up slow platform with a Derby bound slow train. It will remain there until the passage of the next up express, which it will follow south. *Photo H Townley*

Even at country stations the signalling was altered quite extensively over the years. This view shows the down slow platform starting signal in 1952, still a Midland lower quadrant type on a wooden post. Compare this view with the picture in the next pages of 1020 leaving on a down express. There the all the starting signals have distant signals below them, signifying short block. East Buxton box was still open at that time. Once closed the distant signals were all removed because Millers Dale Jct. was the next block. The gantries gave way to single posts. Originally the set back signal off platform two was on a post, but this has been truncated and a doll put on the stump. In the far distance a few wagons can be seen in the entrance of the Station quarry sidings. *Photo L M Hobdey*

An 8F 2-8-0 has run round its spoil train and commences the climb northward. Just where the relaying has been is not known but the collection of brake vans next to the loco, being used as mess vans, indicates there were quite a lot of men involved. The picture was taken from the remains of the kilns of the Station quarry.

Photo Manchester Loco Soc

5XP 4-6-0 45652 "Hawke" runs into Millers Dale with the 9.25am ex Manchester Central in 1954. The photograph taken from the brake van of the Buxton – London through coach. This vehicle has been worked from Buxton coupled to the rear of the 9.30am "pull & push" service. On arrival at Millers Dale the coach was propelled into the yard and uncoupled from the two coaches of the pull & push. The 0-4-4T plus coaches then ran round the through coach so that it was on the bunker end of the loco. On the arrival of the express the coach was attached to the rear, and the passengers proceeded on their way without having to get out of their seats. It was a well patronized service.

Photo L M Hobdey

A rebuilt Crosti boilered 9F 2-10-0 92026 rushes through with a down coal train on July 12th 1965. Scenes like this were soon to become history. The speeds with which these heavy coal trains, with a banker in the rear, came through the station dip was quite startling. The 9F is blowing off, these ex Crosti locos seemed to steam better than the standard single chimney 9Fs, perhaps on rebuilding the blast pipes were modified.

Photo J M Bentley

Millers Dale 1932. A down express departs behind a Midland compound 1020 against the backdrop of the Millers Dale Lime Company's quarry and tip. 1020 was one of the Trafford Park allocated members of this class. The depot originally had numbers 1011-1013, 1015-1022 for its express work to the south. The first two coaches look a little out of place on a Midland division express, by the time this photograph was taken, the pre grouping stock was well mixed up.

Photo E R Morten

Millers Dale 1948. Quite a comparison with the picture of 1020 on the previous page. The two new diesel electric locos 10000 and 10001 depart for Manchester with the 4/35pm ex St Pancras. The photographers have turned out to record this occasion, as it was the first time the locos had worked in multiple on a public service. 10,001 was only just out of the works, as its white roof and bogie frames show. The two locos were tested both singly and in multiple all over the system for years after this picture was taken. ***Photo L M Hobdey***

A Derby light weight DMU drops into the Buxton bay platform to await the next service to Buxton on January 13th 1957. Steam power continued on these turns until October of that year. No man power savings were made by the introduction of these units on this service. The steam hauled trains did not employ a guard, so all that happened was the fireman was exchanged for a guard. Note the new metal signal gantry, the down fast and slow platform starters are now together, the third change of signals over the years. ***Photo H Townley***

Millers Dale June 3rd 1966. A Park Royal rail bus is now working the service to Buxton. This unit arrived at Buxton carrying the "Heads of Ayr" destination indicator, as that was its previous working area. As was usual on the railway at the time, nobody new much about these units, depots found out as they went along. One morning, whilst working the service to Buxton the unit failed at Ashwood Dale and the Sheffield – Buxton freight came up behind to assist it to Buxton. The fireman was somewhat puzzled to find that there were no buffers, after conferring with his driver the class 8F nudged up to the unit so that the fireman could throw the shackle over the hook. A very slow run to Buxton ensued, and on arrival there the waiting fitting staff were horrified to see how the job had been done and the two black greasy dints in the units bodywork It was then explained to all that a bar was carried under the end of the unit for such occasions, but nobody knew about it. The unit retired to the depot whilst a little panel beating was done.
Photo J W Sutherland Manchester Loco Soc

10100 starts a down express away from the station around 1955, on a rather gloomy day. The connecting service for Buxton stands, as usual, in platform 5. The run round road adjacent to this platform used to have a signal arm controlling the exit, but by now this had been replaced by a doll. Also platform 5 had a starting signal on the same gantry as the platform 4 starter. All clearly shown on the previous picture of 1020 departing.   *Photo E R Morten*

5XP 4-6-0 45561 "Saskatchewan" runs in to the station with an up express in 1959. 45561 had been at Bristol for many years and moved to Trafford Park in January 1957, thence to Kentish Town until June 1959 when it came back to Manchester for a short stay until moved back to the London end of the line. This dates the picture to the summer of 1959, as the loco carries a 9E shed plate. The train is only a seven coach job, so it looks like one of the expresses run on XL timings. The load 210 tons will still have kept all concerned busy up to the summit at Peak Forest. *Photo L M Hobdey*

Another 1960 photograph, this time the train is "Britannia" powered. 70015 "Apollo" arrives from Manchester with an up express, made up of Mark 1 stock with headboards. At this time it was possible to see at least four classes of loco on these trains, 5MT, 5XP, Royal Scots and Britannias, all disappeared on the arrival of the Sulzer diesel locos. *Photo L M Hobdey*

45614 "Leeward Islands" rushes in to the station with an up express. I always wondered how the drivers of these expresses stopped just right at the end of the platform. Later, whilst returning home as a passenger off a turn on which we had been relieved at Chinley, I rode on the footplate from there to Millers Dale on one of these expresses. I watched with interest the brake being fully applied on emerging from Chee Tor tunnel, the driver told me he counted to twelve and then put the brake handle back to the off position. We came to a stand with the tender end just on the platform slope. There is no substitute for experience. 45614 was a Kentish Town loco, as the livery might imply. During the summer of 1959 she was loaned to Newton Heath depot. W D Cooper photographed her climbing Shap unassisted with a load of 13 Mark I coaches, well filled with a bank holiday load which must have topped 400 tons by quite a bit. Interesting to note there was not a blow from anywhere, which speaks well for the maintenance of these locos. *Photo E Johnson collection*

46154 "The Hussar" arrives at the head of the up "Palatine" express during its one month stay at Kentish Town depot in May 1959. By June of that year the loco was in residence at Preston depot. *Photo Author's collection*

Millers Dale 1932. The turns between Buxton and Millers Dale were for many years the preserve of the Midland 0-4-4 tank locos, both before and after the introduction of pull and push working, which was introduced in the 1930s. 1366 is seen here attaching a dining car to the rear of an up express. This dining car and its attendants was detached from a down express in an evening, worked to Buxton, where it was cleaned and serviced, and worked back to Millers Dale the following morning. The old bottles and other rubbish from this coach was tipped down the bank between the station and depot at Buxton and, in later years provided a well known bottle hunter with some interesting finds. Driver Gilbert surveys the photographer.   *Photo Author's collection*

Millers Dale 1950. A Webb 5'6" 2-4-2T 46616 is on the Buxton service. These locos often came during the 1930s and 1940s, usually to fill in whilst the Midland type were in the works. 46616 came to Buxton in the late 1940s and remained at the depot until transferred to Swansea in February 1953, and became the last of the class in service. *Photo L M Hobdey*

Millers Dale 1947. Driver Frank Boulton and fireman Gordon Mellor are the crew on the Midland 1P 0-4-4T. 1278. This loco was the las Salter valved member of the class to be at Buxton. On the date of this picture 1278 still carried a 9A Longsight shed plate. The regula allocations still not back to how they were before the war. With the reduction in services, 1278 went to Longsight, where it worked on the Stockport – Stalybridge service.

Photo W D Cooper

Now renumbered 58042 and lettered British Railways, the old 1278 had entered its last phase. A 9D shed plate is now affixed to the smokebox door, but a front number plate is still awaited. Withdrawal came in December 1951, two years after this picture was taken. Buxton still had 58083, 58084 and 46616 to cover this work. All very old locos. 41905 was borrowed frequently to cover absences. No Ivatt 2-6-2T was ever allocated to Buxton, although 41204 did deputise for failed DMUs. Had so many of the Ivatt locos not gone to the Southern region, we might have seen some modern motive power on these turns.

Photo L M Hobdey

Millers Dale 1951. 2P 0-4-4T 41905 propels its two coaches out of the up main platform after detraining its passengers for the next up service. The loco is still carrying the British Railways in extenso on the tanks. 41905 was on loan to Buxton from Longsight.

Photo J Wooliscroft

Millers Dale mid 1950s. Sister loco 41906 departs amid the snow with the Buxton service. In the foreground the rails on the down fast are being changed, between trains, which was the normal way of doing the work. No line closures for this type of work in those days. 41906 was given a general overhaul, complete with a new firebox just before the diesels came and spent most of the next years in store at Buxton. What a good loco for preservation it would have been, but alas the preservation business was a few years away yet.   *Photo W A Brown*

58084 stands at the south end of the Buxton bay platform. This very nice photograph is the only one I have seen taken from this spot. The first building on the right was the old refreshment room. By now just a waiting room, opposite its entrance were the subway steps leading to all the other platforms. The coal in the bunker shows 58084 is on the seven trip middle turn, the loco which did the early turn also covered the late turn, its last trip being the connection for the 6/40 pm from St Pancras. When 58084 was withdrawn in February 1955, it was replaced by a second Stanier 0-4-4T 41906.

Photo Derek Lowe

Freight activities at Millers Dale were quite extensive when the Station Quarry was in operation. The small yard dealt with the quarrys requirements, loads and empties were sorted for picking up by passing freight trains, booked to call in the yard. Quite a deal of household coal for Tideswell, Litton and Cressbrook was dealt with, as well as cattle for local farmers. The goods warehouse catered for the small household and industrial items., Shunting was carried out by jobs from Buxton and Rowsley. These three pictures show a little of the activity. A 1F 0-6-0 2727 is seen shunting sheeted lime wagons. Whilst in 1948 3296 on the afternoon shunter from Buxton sorts the yard out. By this time the quarry was closed, so the sheeted wagon next to the loco will have been picked up at Ashwood Dale quarry on its way down from Buxton. 43290 draws of the down slow platform with wagons for the yard, probably coal whilst 4F 43926 awaits the road with a down goods.

Photos Author's collection and
L M Hobdey

Three views of slow passenger trains stood on platform 3 awaiting the arrival of a down express, which in time honoured fashion they will follow to Chinley, calling at Peak Forest and Chapel-en-le-Frith. This pattern of working never altered, it remained as such right up to the closure of the line. All these pictures were taken by R D Pollard and are reproduced with the permission of the Manchester Loco Soc. A Midland 7ft compound 1022 is the power for this service on May 11th 1935, whilst on June 25th 1937 a Sheffield Millhouses depot 5MT 5042 with a couple of Stanier 57` coaches in the train. The lower picture, the down slow is headed by 1060 one of the early LMS 6'9" compounds, of Derby depot. On the early LMS built members of the class the Midland pattern of the driving position on the right of the cab was retained.

Millers Dale 1948. During the locomotive exchanges the Midland main line over the Peak saw just a couple of the participants. Here one of them covers Millers Dale in smoke. The Southern Railway Pacific loco 34005 "Barnstaple" leaves with a down express for Manchester Central. For the duration of the trials it was fitted with a Stanier 4000 gallon tender with water scoop. The working of this loco over this section caused quite a stir amongst the loco enthusiast fraternity. A considerable number of extra train tickets were sold at Buxton for Millers Dale for the purpose of viewing this spectacle.

Photo L M Hobley

The other loco to work over the Peak during the 1948 exchanges was LNER B1 4-6-0 61254 "Oliver Bury" seen here departing with a down express. The driver off the pull and push stands with pipe in mouth watching the proceedings. As mentioned earlier in the book, this class of loco became a regular sight on this line, taking quite a share in slow train and freight workings.   *Photo E R Morten*

Millers Dale April 1st 1965. A forlorn looking 5XP 4-6-0 45563 "Australia" stands on platform 3 with a down slow train. Bereft of its nameplates and shed plate, a Warrington allocated loco at this time. Withdrawn on November 27th 1965. A sorry sight, which is what the authorities wanted to show, hoping everybody would be pleased to see them go. But this only fuelled the determination of the preservation groups to save as many as possible. Four of the class were saved, 45593, 45596, 45690 and 45699. These will soon be joined by a new build "Patriot" 4-6-0 45551. The greatest sorrow is that the line is not intact to run them on.   *Photo J M Bentley*

Two views of 70042 "Lord Roberts" at Millers Dale working down expresses in 1958. The upper picture shows the loco in the June of that year, just after transfer across London from Stratford to Kentish Town depot. In July it again moved house to Trafford Park, where it was joined by 70004/14 ex Stewarts Lane, 70015/17 ex Old Oak Common and 70021 ex Laira depot Plymouth. 70031 also did a short stint at 9E between 5/1960 and 9/1960. 70032/33 arrived in February 1960. Quite a selection from all over the system. In the lower picture 70042 arrives with the down "Palatine" express. Platform inspector Gordon Riley puts his watch back in his pocket after checking the arrival time.

Photos J Wooliscroft / L M Hobdey

After the clearance for class 7 locos to work over the Midland system, Royal Scot class locos soon appeared on the expresses. Quite a collection of them were shared between Kentish Town, Nottingham and Sheffield Millhouses depots. 46110 "Grenadier Guardsman" enters with the down "Palatine" express on a cold looking January day in 1958. Transferred to 14B in November 1957, 46110 was returned to the western division in June 1958. A white topped Buxton 3 car set awaits the connecting passengers and a suitably attired platform inspector Gordon Riley watches the arrival of the express.

Photo L M Hobdey

A twenty coach empty coaching stock train from Etches Park Derby to Cornbrook carriage sidings Manchester, headed by a Toton 8F 2-8-0 48303 awaits the passage of a down express in 1955. The transfer of stock required for special workings such as northern wakes week traffic, was no small job. It is impossible to imagine nowadays most people going away by train, the northern towns emptying over night, and all returning a week later. Stock, men and locos all needed careful diagramming. It will be a steady plod for 48303 up to Peak Forest summit, as the train is long and heavy.

Photo L M Hobdey

The use of "Crab" 2-6-0s on all classes of train is well recorded. The 245 strong class plus the Stanier variety, were to be found all over the LM and Scottish regions. 42857 of Saltley depot Birmingham works northward with a goods from Washwood Heath to Liverpool or Manchester in 1955. **Photo L M Hobdey**

Another regular goods service was between Rowsley and Trafford Park Manchester. Powered for many years by 3F 0-6-0s. 3612 passes through the station dip before resuming the climb to Peak Forest. 3630 and 3638 were others of the class seen regularly on these jobs. The photographer`s wife and daughter watch the scene from the down main platform No 4. The picture was taken in 1938. **Photo L M Hobdey**

The double heading of passenger trains during the summer season was quite a regular feature over the Peak. 44818 of Derby depot has probably been attached at Derby to assist 5XP 45575 "Madras" with the heavy 10.25 ex St Pancras. Quite often having to draw up at Matlock and Millers Dale, because the train was too long for the platform, was necessary. This caused a little more delay that the hard pressed locos and crews could have done without.   ***Photo Author's collection***

The Nottingham – Liverpool express hauled by 5XP 45636 "Uganda" of Nottingham depot. This service was very handy for people travelling to the Isle of Man. Once on board the train Liverpool Central was the next time the luggage had to be carried. "Uganda" looks quite well cared for by its home depot. Perhaps it was easier to recruit cleaners in Nottingham than in London and Manchester.

Photo L M Hobdey

Rowsley 4F 0-6-0 44017 has been signalled for the up slow line with its train of empty wagons for Rowsley sidings. Running as a class 7 express freight non fitted it never the less has to get out of the way of a more important train. It will stand at the Lime Sidings end of the slow line until its turn comes for departure. The snow and the weather sheet on the loco tell us all we want to know about the weather conditions in the Peak District on this day. *Photo W A Brown*

44565 of Trafford Park depot heads a class 6 goods through the station on June 26th 1961. The train is a Trafford Park – Rowsley service. 44565/66 and 67 were transferred to Trafford Park from Rowsley in January 1960 to cover this work. The driver has put steam on to tighten the couplings in preparation for going over the "knob" at Lime Sidings. *Photo W D Cooper*

Buxton depot's 42942 runs through with the 11.36am Rowsley – Stockport Edgeley goods. The train will be re-marshalled at Buxton, the Stockport traffic going forward on the 1/35pm service. The loco will, after the crew has been relieved, work the 1/30pm Ashbourne goods with whatever traffic it had brought from Rowsley for the "High Peak" line.

Photo L M Hobdey

45616 "Malta G.C. arrives with the down "Palatine" express in 1959. The train consists of 8 Mark 1 coaches. The loco in its usual livery must have been one of the hardest worked members of the class. Later in the day it will return to London with the up "Palatine" express. 45616 was broken up at Crewe on the 30th of January 1961 after running 1,209,630 miles. The loco averaged over 60,000 miles per year during its life.

Photo J Wooliscroft

A Sheffield Millhouses 5MT 4-6-0 5262 departs with an up express, whilst a Derby depot "Crab" 2799 waits to follow with the all stations job to Derby. Both locos well turned out, the 2-6-0 still sporting polished buffer heads. Obviously a summer season picture as the 5MT has no front steam heating pipe. These being removed between May and October each year. *Photo L M Hobdey*

A heavy down special train, needing the services of two locos, passes through the station on August 1st 1938. 4F 0-6-0 4144 piloting a 5MT 2-6-0 no doubt heading for Blackpool or some other resort. The 4F shows all is well in the steam raising department as she flies the flag from the safety valves. *Photo H Townley*

Ivatt 4MT 2-6-0 43033 just recently transferred from Nottingham to Derby depot, runs into platform 3 with a down stopping train in the summer of 1957. The unsightly white patch on the boiler and firebox is from a badly blowing regulator valve. This system of an exterior regulator rod was introduced by Ivatt and later fitted to the British Railways standard classes, was prone to this problem. It was made to look worse by the addition of water softener to the boiler water.

Photo L M Hobdey

45615 "Malay States" a Kentish Town regular arrives with a down express in 1958. One had to admire the way the regular crews on these jobs made these 5XPs steam. The loco has 160 miles behind it and another 5 miles of heavy climbing in front of it, before the swift descent into Manchester.

Photo L M Hobdey

70042 "Lord Roberts" looking very smart arrives with an up express in 1958, not long after its arrival in the area. The class 4 tank stood at the far end of platform 2 has just arrived from Buxton to await the 2/25pm ex St Pancras, which will leave the through coach which it will duly work to Buxton at 5/36pm.
Photo L M Hobdey

A not so clean 70014 "Iron Duke" departs with an up express. The four bolts on the smoke deflectors used to secure the arrow when this loco was working the "Golden Arrow" express. 70014 was the spare engine to cover 70004 on this prestigious train. Not long after this photo was taken 70014 was overhauled at Crewe, returning in all its glory to Trafford Park depot, only to finish up in the canal because of a slip up whilst being moved on the depot. She looked a rather bedraggled and mud covered mess.
Photo L M Hobdey

Another Trafford Park Britannia 70021 "Morning Star" awaits the "right away" with an up express not long after its transfer from Plymouth. The loco has not had the smoke deflector handrails replaced by hand holes like most of the GW allocated members of the class had.

Photo L M Hobdey

A snowy scene at Millers Dale. A brand new 9F 2-10-0 92166 heads a class 5 goods through the snow in the winter of 1958. This loco and 92165 and 92167 were fitted with mechanical stokers and were allocated to Saltley depot Birmingham. The trio were used on the night express goods to Carlisle.

Photo R Bradshaw

LMS 3cyl compound 4-4-0 928, one of the last batch to be built, arrives with a down express in the mid 1930s. By this time the LMS was well saturated with these locos and on arrival in office, William Stanier cancelled the building of the last planned batch. After the war years, with the advent of so many 5MT 4-6-0s the compounds were relegated to slow train working, a form of work which did not suit them. They were principally designed for express working, a job they did well. The withdrawal of the Midland variety started in the late 1940s, most disappearing by 1953. The LMS type were withdrawn steadily from 1952 to 1960, many being stored out of service for quite a while before withdrawal.

Photo E R Morten

Millers Dale circa 1890. A very pleasant view of the original station and part of the village with Knot Low in the background. The "Railway" public house has had an extension and a face lift. The mill still operates its water wheel, encased in a wooden shed. Animal feed sacks are drying on the wall opposite the mill. Local farmers brought oats etc. to the mill to be ground down for animal feed. A Kirtley 0-6-0 passes through the station with an up goods train. Quite an idyllic scene, soon to be disturbed by the building of viaduct No2 and the enlargement of the station.

The station staff at Millers Dale pose for the photographer. A picture taken prior to the station enlargement in 1904.

Photo Author's collection

128

The station staff pose again for the photographer, this time after the station enlargement, thus a larger staff are now required to run the job. They are standing just by the steps to the subway on platform No1. *Photo Author's collection*

A view looking south after the station enlargement and the building of the second viaduct. The work scars are already starting to disappear. The steps outside the "Railway" public house must have caused quite a few broken bones over the years. Not a good feature to negotiate when one is a little inebriated. *Photo Author's collection*

Millers Dale September 1904. An interesting photograph of the construction of viaduct No 2. Taken from the hill on the Wormhill side of the station. A vertical boilered crane runs on a specially laid track in the left foreground. Whilst a hand powered crane sits on top of the wooden beams in the centre of the picture. In the background the kilns of the Oldham Lime Firms Company are still of the open top variety. The scar made by the quarrying is beginning to show by this date.

Photo Rowsley Association

A class 9F 2-10-0 passes over the second viaduct with a south bound goods in the last couple of years of the lines operation. The design and build of the second viaduct contrasted very much with the original structure.

Photo G Alsop collection

A Johnson 2-4-0 has been photographed passing over the old viaduct with an up passenger train in the late 1890s. The photographer has positioned himself on the road from Millers Dale to Litton. *Photo G Waite*

Many years later, in the early 1930s, Ray Morten positioned himself on the quarry tip to get this shot of 13088 crossing the old viaduct with a down Blackpool special train. The stone pillars of both viaducts are similar but the associated steel work very different. The delicate arched metal work of the old viaduct contrasting with the box girder construction of the new viaduct.

This beautiful study of the old viaduct, taken by a Walsall photographer, Mr H Shedden in 1892. It is printed from a ¼ plate glass negative, still in the original wooden storage box in which it has spent the last 122 years and still printing very well. This wonderful collection of 50 negatives has had no scientific preservation or even archival plastic jackets. *Photo E Talbot*

Millers Dale 1937. Ex LNW G1 0-8-0 9032 rolls slowly towards platform 4 obviously awaiting the road northwards, with a goods for Buxton or over Peak Forest. Some 20 years later 49428 of Longsight depot heads a Rowsley-Buxton goods towards the station. The loco is fitted with a tender cab, a good thing in the winter, but awful in the warmer weather, when an already very hot cab was made much hotter. Note the brew can, no doubt with water or cold tea being kept cool between the tender cab and the tender side. *Photos L M Hobdey*

Banking engines were as much a feature on this section of line as were expresses and slow passenger trains. Rowsley depot was kept very busy supplying motive power for these duties. 4F 0-6-0 44334 of that depot is seen here giving of its best behind a train of 40 of slack coal which had another 4F 0-6-0 in front. The loading of freight trains in the Peak District was governed by wagon coupling strength, and what a 20 ton guards brakevan could hold on these gradients if the coupling broke between the loco and the first wagon. So one could come off Rowsley depot with a 4F and take 26 loads of mineral unassisted, in what was termed a single train. Another wagon meant that a banker was required. 26 loads was a good train for a 4F, but if one had a few more wagons and a class 9F you would have to have a banker because of coupling strength. This was a costly operating system which Dr Beeching would not tolerate. This fact caused him to recommend the withdrawal of freight over this section and the complete closure of Rowsley yard. Surely a few fitted wagons would have made a world of difference, not only with stopping the trains, but to allow single trains to be increased in size by a fitted head next to the loco and 26 non fitted behind which the brakevan could hold in the event of a break loose. **_Photo L M Hobdey_**

To help with the provision of banking locos, Rowsley would quite often use locos making their way back to their home depots after a visit to Derby Works. 42308 is being used to bank a train, probably to Buxton, as the loco was allocated there at this time. 42308 moved to Birkenhead in September of 1956, thence to Chester LNW in February 1957 and finally Chester Northgate in July 1957, from where it was withdrawn in the summer of 1959, the first member of the class to be withdrawn. **_Photo L M Hobdey_**

Two aerial of the Millers Dale Lime Firms quarry and sidings. The picture shows that the quarry did not have proper road access, a fact that probably hastened its closure. A train is in the process of being marshalled for the south. Another train departed from here to Northwich at 9/55 pm. A very clear period was required on the main line at Lime Sidings for all these moves to take place, as portions of the train had to be left on the main line whilst the other portions were attached.

Photos La Farge / Tarmac

The remains of Millers Dale as they were on April 12th 1969. Tracks remain intact and not too late for common sense to prevent their removal. As previously mentioned the effect the closure of this line had on the roads in the Peak District is now being felt more than ever. The arrival of 38 ton lorries on our very inadequate roads is being suffered by all and the roads are, despite efforts by the authorities, a mass of pot holes and sunken grids. The slightest bit of bad weather brings us to a standstill. With a new continental terminus at St Pancras, the North West of the country is denied direct access to it by virtue of 12 miles of missing track. No doubt another survey would cost more than the building of the original line, but nothing like the sums of money involved with HS 2. *Photo J W Sutherland Manchester Loco Soc*

MILLERS DALE FOR TIDESWELL STATIONMASTERS

Opened 1st June 1863 as Millers Dale. Renamed Millers Dale for Tideswell 1st May 1889.

From	To	Name	Comment
05.01.1864 **	15.11.1864	Thomas Turner	From Foreman Porter Bradford. To SM Kibworth. [** = official appointement date. Replaced at Bradford 18.08.1863, so in situ earlier, and possibly for the opening of the station.]
15.11.1864	1865	William Fry	From Foreman Porter Colne. To SM Otley
17.10.1865	by 04.1870	William Palmer	From SM Brightside. To SM Thrapston.
c.1869	after 04.1871	William Renals	From SM Gresley. To SM Leagrave.
by late 1871	05.11.1872	Henry Lewis	Possibly from Armley. To SM Upton-on-Severn.
05.11.1872	31.07.1898	William Whitmore	From Passenger Guard Leicester. Retired, aged 67, after 45 year's service. Received gratuity of £50. [in 1881 census aged 50 born Waton, Leicestershire. Wife died during previous year.]
16.08.1898	18.02.1904	Joseph Henry Clarke	From SM New Mills. To SM Matlock. [in 1901 census aged 48, born Sutton Bridge, Lincs.]
1904?	c.07.1908	William E. Coates	From Relief SM Bristol. To SM Kegworth.
c.07.1908	after 01.1921	John Alderson	From Relief SM Sheffield. [in 1911 census aged 36, born Kirkby Thore, Westmorland.]
by 01.1922	after 1924	Albert C. East	From SM Didsbury.